Looking east toward Yonge Street and College Park, formerly
Eaton's College Department Store.
Photo: Vincenzo Pietropaolo

College and Spadina (Sept. 14, 1925). Photo: TA

The Terrence Donnelly Centre for Cellular and Biomolecular Research, 160 College, designed by Behnisch Architects with architects Alliance. Photo: Mark Fram

Three men rest in a field at what is now Spadina Avenue.
Photo: TPL

College and Spadina, looking west (1927). Photo: TA

College, looking east from Bathurst (1902). Photo: TA

College Street – Little Italy

College looking west from Bellevue (circa 1960s). Photo: TA

College Street – Little Italy
Toronto's Renaissance Strip

EDITED BY DENIS DE KLERCK & CORRADO PAINA

Designed by Bryan Gee

MANSFIELD PRESS | CITY BUILDING BOOKS

Library and Archives Canada Cataloguing in Publication

College Street, Little Italy : Toronto's Renaissance strip / edited by
Denis De Klerck and Corrado Paina ; with a foreward by Joe Pantalone ; and
essays by Giulanna Colalillo … [et al.].

ISBN 1-894469-27-5

1. Italian Canadians – Ontario – Toronto – History. 2. College Street
(Toronto, Ont.) – History. I. De Klerck, Denis II. Paina, Corrado, 1954-
III. Colalillo, Giuliana

FC3097.9.I8C64 2006   971.3'54100451   C2006-903084-7

Design: Bryan Gee for Mansfield Creative

Front and back cover colour photo courtesy of Michael Awad
Front and back cover background photos: College Street looking
west and east from firehall tower (1911), by William James,
courtesy of City of Toronto Archives

The publication of this volume was made possible in part by a grant from
the Mariano A. Elia Chair in Italian Studies at York University.

The book has also been generously supported by the Canada Council
for the Arts and the Ontario Arts Council.

Mansfield Press Inc.
25 Mansfield Avenue, Toronto, Ontario, Canada M6J 2A9
Publisher: Denis De Klerck
www.mansfieldpress.net

College and Bathurst, southwest corner (1937). Photo: TA

World Cup crowds (1970). Photo: Vincenzo Pietropaolo

The making of the film *Franco: The Story of an Immigrant*, directed by
Salvatore Greco, on College Street (1975).
Photo: Vincenzo Pietropaolo

The Power store between Clinton and Grace on the north side of College. Photo: Scotiabank Group Archives

TABLE OF CONTENTS

College and Yonge (1916).
Photo: TA

Introduction

JOE PANTALONE

College Street and Little Italy in particular have shaped countless lives as a settlement area for immigrants from across the world. This area, where I have lived for 40 years with my children, my friends and my neighbours, is unique, yet its history provides a great example of the promise and welcome Toronto gives to all of its residents. When I arrived as a 13-year-old son of sharecroppers, from an old-world town in southern Italy, I found a home and community that was vibrant, diverse, somewhat daunting and yet welcoming. It gave me my first English language lessons and my first jobs; it allowed me, as city councillor and Deputy Mayor, to have the honour and privilege of working in public service on behalf of the community for over 25 years. During those years I have met many remarkable people and heard many stories, yet as this book shows so well, there is a deeper history to the street that is fascinating if you scratch a little below the surface.

In this book, Toronto's "renaissance strip" comes alive, thanks to editors Denis De Klerck and Corrado Paina, by showing us how often College Street has been reborn and reinvented. The essays gathered here are scholarly, yet personal. This is a history of a place influenced by immigration cycles set off by world events, but it is also the story of the individuals who are too often left out of history books. In the wonderful photographs that accompany the essays, we can see vivid proof that the buildings and streetscapes of the city are always changing, yet what has remained constant is the evolving creativity and commitment of the people who have made their lives here. For every story that is told, there are countless others that have not been told, because the life of College Street has been so rich and various. This book is a reflection of that richness – it shows us as we were and as we are. It is a gift that will allow future generations to know a little bit more about ourselves.

Enjoy the book!

Joe Pantalone
Deputy Mayor

LEFT: The Pantalone family.
Photo courtesy of Joe Pantalone
RIGHT: Corner of Grace and College.
Photo: Vincenzo Pietropaolo

Café Diplomatico.
Photo: Vincenzo Pietropaolo

The Renaissance Strip

DENIS DE KLERCK & CORRADO PAINA

Toronto will not be a fine town when it is finished.
It is a fine town because it is unfinished.
– JOE FIORITO, Union Station

Walking across the major streets of Toronto can be like sailing on the bed of a river. There are some sections with no particular physiognomy – bland storefronts followed by windswept parking lots with only the occasional relief of a church or public building to mark the architectural ambitions of an earlier age. One has to proceed head down, along blind concrete walls, past plain and homogenized store windows – the mute rows of buildings no more distinct than the sidewalk that winds through the nondescript communities. Eventually the human river turns into vivid, colourful neighbourhoods that appear like sheltering bays, and one can pause within an enclave of warmth and life. Here at the centre and beating heart of human creativity and labour, both visitor and inhabitant can find peace and rest, as well as leisure.

College Street's Little Italy is one of these bays. This free minuscule state becomes the eponym of the street, so that the whole of College becomes Little Italy, despite the large Portuguese presence, just as Danforth is Greek and Bloor is the Annex. This collective imagery is unfair, considering that within a few blocks Bloor contains Korea Town as well as the upmarket stretch around Yorkville. Toronto is a city of perennial immigration and arrival, and its main streets have a habit of forming neighbourhood clusters that are both hamlets of identity and universal breath. To live on College, for most Torontonians, is to picture the Little Italy neighbourhood, though College goes a good way beyond it.

In the 1950s and '60s, when Little Italy was not yet called Little Italy, life had a different rhythm. With the exception of occasional excitements, like the bank-robbing Boyd Gang shooting up College Street, life was pretty quiet. There were few entertainment venues, but lots of fruit and vegetable stores, local butchers, bakers and more traditional shops that sold clothing, shoes and everyday necessities to mostly working-class locals. One could get fresh groceries and drink a good coffee, but fashionable people lining up at local nightclubs were not yet even imagined.

The area was a mix of immigrant groups that were sympathetic to each other. Cohen's Fish Market at the corner of Clinton and College had two frontages, with "Cohen's" written on the College window and the Italian word "pescheria" on the Clinton side. This intimate and easy mix of cultures was exemplified by a local doctor named Joseph Fenton, who lived in the neighbourhood with his wife, Mindie, and their family. Dr. Fenton attended Harbord Collegiate and graduated from the University of Toronto medical school in 1949. Growing up at Bathurst and College, he was a true child of the neighbourhood; as an adult he worked close to home and became an old-school general practitioner, making house calls to his patients, who were largely of Italian and Portuguese descent, and walking everywhere with his familiar black medical bag.

By the '70s, the ethnic mix of this village life was changing; the large local Jewish population had mostly moved out of the area or would soon be going. Eastern Europeans living on Gore Vale and Bellwoods would still come up to shop on the street, but they too began to move on or blend their presence into their surroundings. Most visibly and identifiably at that time, the pocket was inhabited by an established and aging population of Italian and Portuguese immigrants.

Some will say that though there were few restaurants, there was more personality; the neighbourhood was quieter, with only rare visitors from the suburbs. The area functioned more like a village in Italy or in Portugal, with bakeries, butcheries and bars where seniors and hungry youth got together to play out the mortal game of boredom and dispossession. With the exception of special visits to the old Capriccio restaurant or first communion lunches at La Festa banquet hall, it was a working life, and dinner was observed with family at home rather than with friends in restaurants. Religious life had its own fixed schedule and more than a few in the neighbourhood knew the saints' days and attended mass on Sundays at St. Francis of Assisi church or St. Agnes. In the documentary *St. Bruno, My Eyes as a Stranger*, by filmmaker Peter Lynch, Bruno Crescia recollects the times when the neighbourhood was tough and Italians in the know walked only on the north side of College.

But a silent revolution (that would eventually become noisy for the local inhabitants) was taking place in Little Italy. As with many revolutions, the seeds of change were sown when uncontrollable economic events transformed a way of life. On College it began in the '70s, when the New Method laundry closed down and the Steinberg's grocery store took its place. Steinberg's was the first full-sized

Cohen's Fish Market windows at Clinton and College (1969). Photos: Vincenzo Pietropaolo

Dr. Joseph Fenton as a young man.
Photo courtesy of Barry Fenton

modern grocery store in the neighbourhood and has survived to this day under the name Dominion. The convenience of one-stop shopping effectively ruined the many small mom-and-pop grocery stores that used to line College. When the Dufferin Plaza was roofed over and became an indoor mall with equally ample parking – with heat in the winter and air conditioning in the summer – the small clothing and shoe stores on College began to die off one by one as customers traded personal allegiances for corporate convenience.

An area in decline cannot have a successful revolution and renaissance without the work of a few creative individuals who plant their own seeds of change. They thrived before the decline and they helped reverse it. In 1959, the Sicilian Ice Cream Café at the corner of College and Montrose was established by the Galipo family as the first Italian café and gelateria. It was an important meeting place for the neighbourhood and, moreover, it brought a concept of public leisure and pleasure to the street. The Galipos' success was such that their ice cream is still sold all over Toronto and neighbourhood children are brought there by parents who were themselves brought there as children. When the Mastrangelo family opened Bar Diplomatico at College and Clinton in 1969, their patio set another precedent for the kind of café culture that Little Italy would become known for in the '90s.

Another huge influence on the identity of Little Italy

Joe Rauti as Christ. Photo courtesy of Joe Rauti

The Way of the Cross

As with so many good things in life, the Way of the Cross – the procession that winds its way through Little Italy every Good Friday – began almost by accident.

It all started in 1962, when Vito Telesa, sacristan at St. Agnes Church, stumbled upon a statue of Christ in the church's closet. The discovery inspired St. Agnes' friars and several young parishioners – fresh off performing in an Easter play – to carry the statue out into the streets in celebration.

Since then, this once-tiny parade has continued to grow with every passing year, attracting bigger crowds and more participants. And when the Italian community moved from St. Agnes to St. Francis of Assisi Catholic Church in the late 1960s, so did the procession.

Today, the parade still features many statues in the lineup, but the big draw for believers (and non-believers alike) is the over 200 real-life, costumed volunteers portraying religious figures such as Mary, Joseph of Arimathea, Mary Magdelene, Judas and the Apostles. Although procession volunteers are always honoured to take part in any role, the biggest role of them all – Jesus – is not up for grabs. For the serious acting that is required in scenes such as the flagellation of Christ, St. Francis has turned to only one man, Joe Rauti, for the past 33 years.

Today, the Easter procession boasts the claim of being the largest of its kind in all of North America.

The original Diplomatico patio.
Photo: Rocco Mastrangelo

was the creative spirits of Severino and Giovanna Manni. Beginning with Severino's barbershop on Clinton (and a second shop on College), they were responsible for creating Festival Variety, which still exists, the iconic Il Gatto Nero – co-owned with Carmine Raviele, who eventually bought it and continues to run it with his son Michael – Masaniello, which was for many years one of the few fine dining restaurants on the street, and finally Giovanna's, which is still family run with the help of their son Salvatore and daughter Lucia. Similarly Vincenzo Bertucci began in the '50s with a lunch counter at College and Dovercourt. Later he would open Il Risorgimento, a billiard hall that served some of the first espresso on the street. Upstairs was La Festa banquet hall, which hosted weddings and first communions and attempted for a while to bring jazz music to the street. The music never really caught on, but in the '90s, Vincenzo's son Domenic, an expert sommelier, would open Bertucci's, a fine dining restaurant with an extensive wine list. This marked a necessary evolution of a new generation of restaurateurs. Like those of the Bertuccis, the Galipos, the Mastrangelos and the Mannis, the businesses that most influenced contemporary College Street are still family run and their success has inspired more than a few successful imitators. Even businesses that were not family run had familial lineages as partnerships formed and split up, with one partner moving down the street to start fresh. Eventually all of this cell

L to R: Giovanni DiSalvo, Vito Orlando, Franco Maranzan, Severino Manni, Nick Mastrogiovanni. Photo courtesy of Severino Manni

The Bitondos in their shop on Clinton Street.
Photo: Vincenzo Pietropaolo

The Monarch Hotel at Clinton and Henderson, circa 1940s.
Photo courtesy of the Pimpinella family.

division and growth resulted in a Little Italy that has become synonymous with café culture for most Torontonians.

Though the bars and restaurants were visible markers of the public life of Little Italy in the early days, the renaissance came out of a neighbourhood cohesion that was formed through the early work of many community leaders. People like G. Branca Gomes, John Medeiros, Nivo Angelone, Gino Ventresca, Giuseppe Simonetta, Fortunato Rao, Giuseppe Frascá, Professor Frank Mazzotta, Vincenzo Bertucci and Leonardo Cianfarani contributed to the cultural life, as well as the working life, of the community, and many of them worked hard to help settle the new wave of immigrants that was beginning to build. COSTI Immigrant Services, founded

by the Italian community in 1952 to serve the needs of immigrants, has become an all-embracing, multicultural social agency that provides educational and employment services to all immigrant communities. St. Stephen's Community House has similarly created social programs and done important community outreach since 1962.

By the early '80s, the College Street that is recognizable today began to take root. Local city councillor Joe Pantalone pushed hard to build the College and Shaw branch of the Toronto Public Library, which helped give the community a cultural focal point not based simply on ethnicity. Johnny Lombardi made a commitment to establish and build the new CHIN Radio and Television headquarters in the

neighbourhood at a time when many businesses were leaving. Lombardi was a great promoter, bringing many Italian entertainers to the area. He once turned Grace Street into the Via Sophia for a visit by actress Sophia Loren. That event shut down College when thousands of fans came out for a glimpse of the screen goddess. Trees were planted along this stretch of College in 1983, and as they took root they began to shade an increasingly diverse local population.

By this time the restaurateurs Eugene Barone, Andrew Milne-Allan and Giancarlo Carnevale opened Trattoria Giancarlo, bringing an entrepreneurial spirit to the neighbourhood that grafted the traditions of the past onto a new reality that was transforming the street. The exodus

Boccette players at the original Bar Italia.
Photo: Vincenzo Pietropaolo

Eugene Barone and Andrew Milne-Allen shooting pool with a new mix of patrons at the original Bar Italia.
Photo courtesy of Eugene Barone

of many Italians to the far reaches of York Region was balanced by an influx of single professionals, young families, artists and students. This was the beginning of the end of the old College Street. In the early '80s, you could still wake to the sound of a rooster strutting in a nearby yard, or more uncomfortably, hear the shrill screams of rabbits raised for slaughter and bred on a roof above a nearby Portuguese butcher shop. Chickens in the backyard didn't disappear out of fear of law enforcement; it was simply that the generation that had felt it was natural to raise their own food had begun to leave. They were soon replaced by people attracted to the village atmosphere, paradoxically, because it was only a few short steps to downtown.

A new wave of restaurants and bars with more sophisticated food and music was beginning to appear, and for the first time the area became a destination for people who lived outside the neighbourhood. When Barone bought an old pool hall named Bar Italia and introduced an innovative menu by Andrew Milne-Allan, his success ignited a fuse that exploded into an entire entertainment district.

A big part of the charm of the first Bar Italia was its mixture of old and new. Opened in 1970s by Bruno Tassone, it was an old-style pool hall where women never ventured and men played pool and cards and debated the sporting events of the day. Up and down College were similar sports bars, and after dinner in the summer the men would gather on the

sidewalk to talk and smoke, slipping inside now and then to drink espresso and bitters.

The Diplomatico, with one of the first and best patios in the city, had become an institution by this time. Il Gatto Nero, which changed locations twice – first from the south side to the north side of College and then from College near Beatrice to College and Montrose – was renowned for its espresso. But it was really the clientele that started the metamorphosis that would modernize College. The owners of these restaurants and bars became, consciously or unconsciously, the promoters of an area that went from serving the famous sandwiches of San Francesco, Bitondo and California to serving genuine Italian and international cuisine. More

Francesco Galle. Photo: Rick O'Brien

Friends at the Bar Sport. Photo courtesy of Joe Pantalone

Greg Davis at Soundscapes. Photo: Rick O'Brien

Aurelio Galipo at Sicilian Ice Cream Café.
Photo courtesy of Galipo family

FROM LEFT: Giuseppe Simonetta, Joe Pantalone,
Art Eggleton and Tony Porretta.

Novelist Liz Brady. Photo: Denis De Klerck

Prime Minister Pierre Elliott Trudeau campaigns in Little
Italy for Jim Coutts. Photo courtesy of Joe Pantalone

Giuseppe and Teresa Andaloro, Rimini Family Clothing.
Photo courtesy of Andaloro family

FROM LEFT: Nancy Barone, Judy Cade and Bruce
Cockburn (circa 1980s). Photo: Gianna Patriarca

Easter Procession with Giuseppe Simonetta.
Photo courtesy of Joe Pantalone

Singer Rocco del Sud cheering Italy in the World Cup.
Photo courtesy of Joe Pantalone

Giuseppe Simonetta and Vito.
Photo courtesy of Joe Pantalone

Krista Tobias at Ted's Collision & Body Repair.
Photo: Rick O'Brien

The Queen Mother drops by St. Mary Magdalene Church
for a visit. Photo courtesy of Father Harold J. Nahabedian

Andrew Milne-Allen and Giancarlo Carnevale, owners of
Trattoria Giancarlo. Photo courtesy of Gianna Patriarca

Eugene Barone, Denis De Klerck and Ruth Gewurtz at the
original Bar Italia. Photo courtesy of Eugene Barone

College and Clinton. Photo: Mark Fram

and more, the character of the cafés and bars was changing the neighbourhood. Strong coffee, inspiring discussion and affordable prices turned Little Italy into a more inclusive and diverse destination – a crossroads where everyone was welcome. It was striking to see a place where seniors of Italian and Portuguese background stopped for an espresso with a new generation from different walks of life. It is more striking that the two parts – one of old immigrant origin and one of students, intellectuals and professionals of every background – could exist together in a sympathetic relationship.

Artists had begun to inhabit the neighbourhood in larger numbers by the '80s, attracted by its aura of "authenticity," good coffee and ready conversation, and the delicious sense one gets by discovering a special place that locals know has been there all along. Bruce Cockburn lived on the west side of Clinton overlooking the Diplomatico and Lorraine Segato was living a few doors down the street on College when she heard her Queen Street West band, the Parachute Club, hit the airwaves with their anthem "Rise Up" for the first time. Artists Robert Fones and Lynn Donoghue were among countless others who began their day with a coffee and a little community conversation. As places like Bar Italia and Il Gatto Nero became more successful, women began to feel much more welcome in the bars along the street that had formerly catered to an almost exclusively male clientele. Once a new clientele of women came, a new clientele of men soon followed. One by one, the old restaurants and sports bars were purchased, often because

a liquor licence was already in place, and the businesses were updated to accommodate changing tastes. By the early '90s, the street began to grow and change at record speed.

Giancarlo Carnevale, whose namesake restaurant is now owned by Tony and Jenny Barato – and is still one of the best restaurants in the city after over 20 years – returned to the street by opening up the College Street Bar with partners Ted Footman, Mark Ferrera and Robert Bowers. Their business was successful thanks to the sophisticated food of Carnevale, served in the unpretentious atmosphere of a neighbourhood restaurant/bar. Like Bar Italia, its business model included restaurant dinner service, and when that was over, the music would be turned up or the band would go onstage, and it would become a bar for the remainder of the night. This model was widely imitated and soon the street was busy until closing hours.

In a short period, the success bred more cell division and growth. Eugene Barone, while retaining Bar Italia, bought the old Capriccio restaurant and turned it into a jazz venue with an ambitious kitchen. In 1995 he opened a new Bar Italia right next door to the old one. The sleek, two-storey venue quickly became a fashionable, standing-room-only bar full of artists and young, well-dressed media types. Nancy Barone opened a beautiful restaurant called Ellipsis down the street. The College Street Bar partners began to have different views of how to run their business, and the partnership split in half, with Robert Bowers and Mark Ferrera heading a few

doors down to open the Midtown. They would eventually open a second restaurant 100 feet away called the Midtown West. Meanwhile, Giancarlo Carnevale bought out remaining partner Ted Footman, and Footman opened up Ted's Collision & Body Repair directly across the street.

As one business morphed into the next, Little Italy became less ethnocentric and less strict about the kinds of businesses that were possible in the formerly quiet neighbourhood. Few people exemplified these changes more than Ted Footman, who has the dubious distinction of introducing haggis to College Street on what became his annual Robbie Burns Day celebration. While Capriccio brought in some of the best jazz in the city – as Bar Italia did later on – and College Street Bar established its long-running "Soul Sundays," Footman introduced musicians and bands like Fred Eaglesmith, Hey Stella and the Wayward Angels. When the city wouldn't let him open up his second floor to expand his business, he simply started another one down the street. The two-storey venue, with Barcode on the main floor and Ted's Wrecking Yard on the second, became another important music venue in the city – it was one of the few places on the street that booked bands that played original music rather than cover tunes.

CONTINUED PAGE 37

Far left: Henderson Ave
Above: The Monarch Tavern
Photos: Bryan Gee

Near left: Antonia Lanni
Photo: Denis De Klerck

Above: Photo Laurence Siegel
Below: Ted Footman, Simon, John.

Ted's Collision. Photo: Rick O'Brien

Performers like Broken Social Scene, Leslie Feist, the Stars, the Sadies and Sum 41 got their first regular gigs there. When swing music made a brief resurgence, Footman booked a 12-piece swing band for weekly dances.

While Footman brought a new variety of music to the street, Bar Italia found a new role as a centre for people interested in books, film and design. *Toro* and *Outpost* magazines held regular editorial meetings there, as did John Knechtel and his *Alphabet City* crew; designer Bruce Mau used the place as a second office; Antonio D'Alphonso and his company Guernica began their regular series of book launches featuring some of the best Italian Canadian writers, providing a touchstone to one of the communities that made such a resurgence possible. On any given day, one could find writers, editors, architects and filmmakers sipping espresso and pretending to work while they caught up on the latest gossip on the street.

Little Italy has always had its share of filmmakers and actors as well. Peter Lynch, Valerie Buhagiar and Bruce McDonald have had a long association with the neighbourhood and were among the first to work out of this environment. And it wasn't only Bar Italia that gave a home to these artists. By the mid-'90s, it seemed that every restaurant employee on the street was an aspiring actor and every second table held someone who was working up a screenplay or a novel, a poetry book or a dance routine. The community of businesses welcomed everyone, and most of them

Kent Nussey

Bruce McDonald

Peter Lynch

ABOVE: **Roland Jean**

BELOW: **Jerry Ciccoritti**

Shooting the Street

PHOTOS: RICK O'BRIEN

College Street has been filmed many times before, but rarely by people who have international stature as artists, as well as a local understanding of the terrain. In the film *A Love Supreme*, based on a novel by Kent Nussey, Bruce McDonald, one of Canada's most celebrated directors, has teamed up with documentary filmmaker Peter Lynch to co-direct a story that is set in the streets that run through the community. Cast and crew are almost all from the neighbourhood; even Jerry Ciccoritti, who directed his own feature film, *Boy Meets Girl*, in Little Italy, plays a small role.

ABOVE: **Christie Macfadyen and Brian Stillar**

LEFT: **Adrien Dorval**

The midnight drag show at El Convento Rico.
Photo courtesy of Christian Aviles

The Big Deal on College Street, an outdoor film
festival on the Grace Street Public School grounds,
shows *Stromboli*, with Ingrid Bergman (1999).

The Boyd Gang's College Street Shootout

Throughout the early 1950s, Toronto was smitten with the Hollywood-style criminal activities of a group of bank robbers. Labelled the "Boyd Gang" by Toronto *Daily Star* crime reporter Jocko Thomas, the illicit heists of the group had Toronto mesmerized.

The gang was comprised of Edwin Alonzo Boyd, the man with "the matinee-idol good looks," Willie "the Clown" Jackson and Lenny "Tough Lennie" Jackson. After escaping from the Don Jail using a hacksaw blade hidden in Lenny's wooden foot, the three men pulled off several robberies, including one of Canada's biggest ever: the theft of over $30,000 from Royal Bank's Leaside branch.

As a drama-hungry media picked up the Boyd Gang lead, the gang's unusual biography quickly became celebrated myth. But the appeal soon turned to fear on March 6, 1952, when two Toronto detectives were shot in a gunfight on College at Lansdowne Avenue. After robbing the Bank of Montreal at College and Manning shortly after 1 p.m., the gang tried to make a quick getaway in a vehicle driven by Lenny and one of their cohorts, Steven Suchan. When officers Edmund Tong and Roy Perry tried approaching the gang's car, they were shot. Perry recovered, Tong didn't.

Put into the Don Jail yet again, Lenny and Suchan tried to make one final escape, but eventually were hanged for their crimes at 12:14 a.m. on December 16, 1952.

understood the importance of providing a forum for the arts community. The Hot Docs film festival, established in 1992, used to screen its films in the many restaurants on the street. It has since grown into the largest documentary film festival in North America.

When local poet Margaret Christakos created Poetry College, in 2001, it was once again the restaurants along the street who played host to this innovative festival of the spoken word. What made events like Hot Docs and Poetry College successful was that the first people to attend them were the people who actually lived in the neighbourhood – these events thrived because the organizers paid attention to the local community. Restaurateurs understood the importance of this community support too. Ted Footman

once hired a 40-piece symphony orchestra to play Beethoven's Symphony No. 5 in the parking lot next to Ted's Wrecking Yard simply because it was a fun thing to share. Similarly, Eugene Barone was the main sponsor of Big Deal on College, an outdoor film festival that ran for three summers, screening Italian movies in the park of Grace Street Public School. Local residents were invited to bring family and friends as well as a blanket and got a free movie and popcorn in return.

Culture is a reciprocal arrangement; many of the cultural enterprises that took place on the street happened because the community that lived there welcomed them. Despite the outwardly conservative appearance of the largely Catholic Italian and Portuguese community, the neighbourhood still welcomed El Convento Rico, a well-known dance club featuring a regular

weekend drag show that was created as a place where the gay and lesbian latino community could feel safe and free to express themselves. The street today has become the mirror and the emblem of today's Toronto – the city of coexistence, of live and let live.

The fortunes of cities and neighbourhoods ebb and flow throughout their histories, and when they are at their peak of cultural creativity it is usually because a spirit is born that is palpable – to be within its energy field is to be prodded and pushed to contribute to its growth. In the '90s, College Street, which began in the previous century as a suburb of Toronto, became fully integrated with downtown, yet managed to retain enough of its original identity to make it a unique and identifiable place on the cultural map. It has never been simply an entertainment district with nightclubs lining up row on row, leaving it a daytime wasteland. Though the music is turned up late at night and people come out to dance and party, most of

the businesses begin the evening by serving food, providing a place for the community – and it is a large one now – to break bread together and share conversation. The centrality of food and conversation very likely comes out of its joint Italian and Portuguese background, as does the promenade that takes place every summer night when crowds of people walk from Euclid to Shaw and back again, sometimes stopping for gelato, sometimes for coffee. Little Italy becomes an elongated village square at these moments, and children and families are as welcome as the hipsters who dress up for a night on the town. People are not there to window shop as they might in other neighbourhoods, because there is not a strong retail presence on this stretch. They are there to see each other, rather than a store or an event, which is rare enough in Toronto to make it remarkable.

In the first years of this new century, Little Italy has somehow managed to become an entertainment district while

retaining much of its village atmosphere, especially in the daytime. The procession on Good Friday is a classic example of this syncretic existence, when seniors and their families who remained in the area join new settlers in a rite that is religiously solemn and socially festive. It is not the religious moment that unifies, but the processional element that makes all inhabitants actors as well as witnesses. Though it is one of the largest processions of its kind in North America, it remains an intimate community gathering. People who long ago left the neighbourhood for the manicured lawns of suburbia return on this day to reminisce and meet up with old friends. It has become an important event for aspiring politicians to be seen at because it draws some of the most important community leaders in the city – without their blessings, the door to political office remains only half-open.

There are still seniors here who stop in the park before going to mass, and like disciples of Saint Francis, talk to the seagulls

Saturday Night on College Street.
Photos: Bryan Gee

and pigeons while tossing bread scraps and leftovers from last night's pasta. They still stare curiously, like they used to in their villages and towns, at the arrival of a stranger, at the actors and filmmakers who come out of the Royal Cinema or the people who leave the restaurants only to hang out on the sidewalk. The two insular worlds don't collide but rotate around one another, and the children of the new families of Little Italy run readily to the old men and women who ask them their names in broken English. There are still seniors who play cards at the Caravelle club or bocce in the summer at Bickford Park, who walk in the evening like they used to in Italy or Portugal, repeating the liturgy of the *struscio* (touching, walking), who stop on the sidewalks or at the corner of Grace and College where a bronze Johnny Lombardi sits evangelically explaining life to a curious boy. They talk about soccer and politics in their old countries while young people run nervously around them to Revival or the Mod Club or the many other venues where music and

nightlife breathe convulsively.

This is the area where much has happened and anything can happen, where any morning one can go to the grocery store and fight with Italians and Portuguese who palpate fruit before buying it or steal a few grapes to test their quality. At the same time there are children running on the sidewalks to school, past the debris of a wild night before. Despite everything, one can have one's righteous sleep at night even as somebody else is waking up.

College Street is a microcosm of Toronto, built out along dirt roads with horse and cart until streetcars and cars came along and, with them, so many people from all over the world. Their lives were not so different from ours; they were going to work, they were coming back tired, and the light of the same sun was flooding over the roofs of the city. New lives begin, though the old ones are unfinished, yet nothing much has changed in the end on College Street, in Little Italy.

College looking west from Bellevue (circa 1960s). Photo: TA

Digging for the Garrison Creek sewer (circa 1890s).
Photo: TA

19th-century Suburbia
21st-century Cool

(or How to Build a City Street)

MARK FRAM

Two men rest in a field at
what is now Spadina Avenue.
Photo: TPL

Toronto is an east-west city. That is, you locate yourself in street numbers east and west from Yonge, which claims to be Canada's longest street. There is otherwise only north – "up" from Lake Ontario.

Unusually for an east-west strip, College Street has no "east" from Yonge, although for many decades it has suffered the minor indignity of accommodating the *Carlton* streetcar, which began and flourished as the *College* car and which also wanders along Gerrard and other streets. College Street goes only west – from what might have been the world's biggest department store, through a hodgepodge of institutions, former factories, street commerce, apartments, houses, schools and churches until finally (poetically, inevitably) one last burger joint. And although it was intended to be a straight main route, halfway between the original colonial arteries surveyed along Bloor and Queen streets, College spreads out and wiggles a little bit on its way, offering tantalizing clues about its past and maybe its future.

The perfect streetcar strip

Big cities are often seen and valued through their networks of main commercial thoroughfares. To begin with, today's main-street shopping strips are emblematic of the industrial-capitalist city of the 19th century. Each bit of street is the location of small businesses and large; the setting for political struggles of frontier settlements to get big-city services; the transportation route along which most everyone moved and still does; and the backdrop for both

the ostentation of the rich and the supposed indignity of the poor.

On commercial streets like College, the technological innovations of the 19th and 20th centuries are most rapidly and publicly displayed, and their surviving traces are most easily picked out. College Street was developed as a streetcar strip, powered by the newfangled technology of electricity. Today it remains a streetcar strip, despite the grumbling of car drivers. Other major locations that were transformed in the 19th century, such as the household interior and the factory floor, are much less publicly conspicuous.

Once you pay close attention, every commercial street in the city is distinctive: close up, College is quite different from nearby Dundas, Bloor or Queen. A commercial strip often carries a distinct image of its particular locality, because it mixes up a variety of building types, not just houses. It's also more literally public: College (like its siblings) is both neighbourhood spine and neighbourhood barrier by virtue of its traffic, with different influences and histories discernible in the architecture and patterns of use on its frontages.

And, despite ongoing change, the essential function of a commercial street like College – accommodating the movement and interaction of people, things and (of course) money – remains a continuing storyline through time that lets us understand the past and the present side by side.

From its start, Toronto wasn't very effectively *planned*. The current city is the result of countless cases of building, rebuilding and making do under the pressure of existing

conditions, both natural and human, with very rare (and expensive) attempts to overcome or override those conditions. Oh, there was certainly the right-angled hand of the surveyor at work on the layout of land grants and farms. But quite unlike Manhattan or Chicago (or Mexico or Beijing) and other well-known examples of the parcelling of land for city-building around the world, the Toronto grid is not one big grid, but a set of tiny grids subdivided over time out of bigger grids – just like hundreds of matryoshkas (those nested Russian dolls).

The original colonial survey before 1800 comprised "concession" roads almost a kilometre and a half apart (100 surveyor's chains, or 6,600 feet, to be more precise): for instance, Queen, Bloor and St. Clair running east to west, and Yonge, Bathurst and Dufferin north to south. Within each big square of this grid, 10 or 20 rectangular lots were doled out or sold as farm lots or elite estates. Since then, each of these big lots has been subdivided and sliced and diced and julienned into bite-sized (well, house-sized) chunks of land and building, sometimes with great inconsistency.

Toronto's grid wiggles: up and down because the land was dissected by ravines, and side to side because the overall pattern of subdivision was executed by people who didn't always cooperate.

The modern map of old Toronto is among the proudest expressions of 19th-century laissez-faire capitalism anywhere. Almost every public space in Toronto had to be clawed back from private hands. College Street has generous width

"Sleepy Hollow" on College between Elizabeth and Queen's Park (1885). Photo: TPL

College Street gates looking west from Yonge (circa 1800s). Photo: TPL

OPPOSITE: Frederick Perkins House at College and St. George (1904). Photo: TPL

The Taddle Ravine at University and College (1888). Photo: TPL

between the University of Toronto and Manning Avenue not because of government foresight, but because the family that laid out the original lots wanted a classier urban district than their much less imaginative neighbours. The checkered history of how the land was laid out set the stage for the variety of what would come to be.

The result: College Street is both main street and corner café. Its workplaces, commerce and housing have grown into a chain of "traditional" neighbourhoods over several decades, with their mixed occupation, form, tenure, scale and even cost. This isn't always an upward trend – some sections of the street are hopping, others less so. College was constructed out of uneven terrain and hundreds of uncoordinated intentions, cycles of development, decline, renewal, and on and on – its parts weren't the same five years ago, and they won't be the same five years from now. College Street is the whole city in summary.

Few of its buildings were designed by professional architects, fewer still by architects known beyond their immediate locale. In the commercial walk-ups, changes in fashion and technique of store layout, lighting and signage, as well as the kinds of goods for sale, have often drastically altered the ground floors. Despite those alterations, the past is often readily discernible on the ground. Their upper storeys, on the other hand, remain remarkably unaffected. This persistence gives many parts of College a strong connection to the era of their origins and early lives. Which is a roundabout way of saying that these places embody the history of the city in a way that other parts cannot.

How to plant a street

Both College Street and University Avenue take their names from the University of Toronto (originally King's College), which had received a land grant to the north of the fledgling town of York in 1827. The grant was a rectangle bounded roughly by Bloor Street and a line halfway between Queen and Bloor, and by the backlots of properties that front on what is now Bay Street to the east and St. George Street to the west. The university's grant also included private driveways east to Yonge Street from its southeast corner (now College Street) and south to the university's gate on Queen Street (originally College *Avenue*, now University). Until 1859, the university forbade public access to its driveways, and there was a parallel city street (Park Lane) alongside the southern drive. The "modern" University Avenue above Queen Street is especially wide because it incorporates both earlier routes.

So, before 1859, there was no public traffic east and west through the university lands between Queen and Bloor, and even though College shows up on maps long before, it didn't begin to carry public traffic until the 1860s. Before Toronto's suburban expansion, this limited accessibility was hardly an issue. Large estates on long, narrow "park" lots fronted on Queen Street, from which individual drives ran northward to serve the country homes of the elite. On the west side of

The Denison Estate (1865).
Photo: AO

The Denison Family

Considered one of the most influential families in the early development of Toronto back when the city was still a town called York, the Denison family has been a political and military powerhouse ever since its patriarch, John Denison, arrived here from England in 1796.

According to history books, Captain Denison immigrated here with his family after a personal invitation from Lord Simcoe to come to the newly formed York. The Denisons' loyalty and sacrifice were aptly rewarded with the reservation of 100-acre park lots in the family's name, lots on which they would build their huge estates and villas, transforming the face of this city forever.

Numerous landmarks and streets in this neighbourhood are named after the Denison family, testaments to their place in this history. Denison Square, Avenue and Creek, Bellevue Avenue, Dovercourt Road, Rusholme Road, and Major, Robert, Borden and Lippincott streets – none of these would have their current names without the Denisons. In fact, Denison Avenue used to be the family's driveway from their house to Queen Street. St. Stephen's-in-the-Field Church, the first Anglican Church west of Spadina, was founded and paid for entirely by Captain John's grandson, Robert Denison. The Kensington Market that we all love and frequent was born out of a Denison family estate, the Belle Vue.

The Denisons made an indelible mark on this neighbourhood – no question about it.

St. Mary Magdalene Anglican Church on Manning Avenue (circa 1890). Photo: TPL

the emerging city, only Bathurst and Dufferin ran all the way between Queen and Bloor.

Some north-south driveways would become city streets: most notably Spadina Avenue, developed by Robert Baldwin. Even though his family lands were still very rural in his lifetime, he anticipated the future city, laying out by 1842 not only Spadina Circle, but expansive 100-foot-wide boulevards for Spadina Avenue, a widened Queen Street east from Spadina, and a wide westward extension of a College Street that didn't yet exist, as far as what is now Major Street.

By contrast, the standard Toronto city street allowance of one surveyor's chain (66 feet, or roughly 20 metres) applied most everywhere else, no matter what the actual role of the street: almost every right-of-way in the original Toronto, from Yonge to a one-block side street, is 66 feet wide.

Even though a public street east to Yonge Street would not appear until the 1860s, the estates of two other major landholders to the west of Baldwin's, the Denisons and the Crookshanks, accommodated the widened College Street further west in 1854, well past Bathurst to what is now Manning. But at Manning the grand urban boulevard of the future came to an abrupt halt. Save for St. Stephen's Church, begun in 1857, this was still mostly open farmland and pasture, and landowners to the west didn't see much of a city coming.

Until the 1860s, the local elites had anticipated a considerable increase in a wealthy merchant class that could afford to

ABOVE: St. Stephen's-in-the-Fields Anglican Church at College and Bellevue (1865). Photo: TPL BELOW: St. Stephen's after the fire (1865). Photo: TPL

RIGHT: Map of Crawford Estate (1885). Photo: TPL
NEXT PAGE: 1876 bird's-Eye view of Toronto. Photo: U of T Libraries

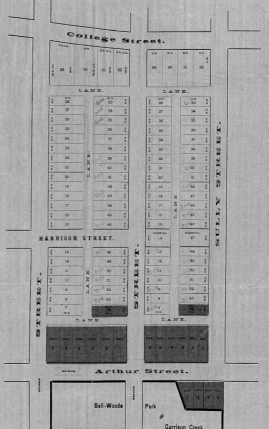

THE
CRAWFORD ESTATE

BEING PART OF PARK LOT 23, TORONTO,

THE PROPERTY OF

THE ONTARIO INDUSTRIAL LOAN & INVESTMENT CO.

THE rapid and, in fact, extraordinary growth of Toronto westward, induced the present proprietors a few years ago to acquire and lay before the Public in building lots of suitable size, the fine tract of land shown on this plan. Noticeable as was the growth of the City in this neighbourhood at that time, what must be said of it now? Whole fields of waste land which not so long ago could be seen between Bathurst street and Parkdale have given place to well-paved streets and avenues, filled with sightly and substantial buildings.

To the intending investor the question must suggest itself —How long is it safe to postpone making a selection? Everybody must admit that now is the time to invest in West End Real Estate; land which could have been bought three years ago at $12 per foot cannot to-day be had for less than $20 or $25, and everything warrants the anticipation of a like increase in the future.

The onward march of the City of Toronto is assured; its Real Estate was never better worth purchasing than it is to-day.

In the property before you it is claimed there is every imaginable quality requisite for a desirable dwelling site.

Crawford street, forming the central line, is pleasantly situated, overlooking, as it does, the attractive grounds of Trinity College, and running through the picturesque Bellwoods Park. The street having recently been block-paved, citizens will find it a pleasant drive along Crawford street and over the bridges which span the Garrison Creek ravine. Along this ravine and following the creek has been constructed the famous Garrison Creek sewer, over which it is proposed to form a public drive, in accordance with the scheme for parks and drives formulated by ex-Mayor McMurrich.

The work of bridging and grading Shaw street north to College street, will shortly be commenced; when completed this will make one of the handsomest avenues in the City.

As will be seen by the plan, the Street Cars pass quite close to the property.

☞ Special inducements will be offered to investors during the fall of 1885.

Terms liberal and made to suit purchasers.

For full information apply at the office,

TORONTO ARCADE, 24 Victoria Street,
or in the evening to Mr. LIGHTBOURN, 77 Crawford Street (on the property).

Ontario Industrial Loan & Investment Co.

J. GORMLEY,
Managing Director.

The Property and Picturesque Grounds of Trinity College.

TRINITY COLLEGE, TORONTO.

Prittle Ravine ran north-south between Roxton and Shaw (1913). Photo: TA

Crawford Street Bridge (Aug. 1, 1912). Photo: TA

The old Harbord Street Bridge at Bickford Ravine (1910). Photo: TA

Garrison Creek

Dips and turns in our streets, roars and gurgles beneath the ground – sights and sounds we experience every day that hint at the remnants of Toronto's biggest buried treasure right here in our neighbourhood.

Garrison Creek, six kilometres of waterway about 12,000 years old, would've allowed you to paddle in a tiny boat from Christie Pits all the way to Fort York, if it were still above ground. But it has been relegated to the ground beneath our feet, flowing under our homes, parks, streets, stores and schools. Beginning in the mid-1900s, it was gradually filled, covered over, routed through, encased in brick – the method may have varied along different sections of its winding path, but the end result was always the same.

The only way we can see Garrison Creek now is to look at features above the ground, which still say volumes about the creek's impact on the shape of this city. Side streets along College, like Crawford and Roxton, that drop and dip, valleys once that have been built up and paved over with concrete now. Houses that lined up like rows of crooked teeth, as some have described, tilting because their shallow foundations have slowly set into mushy grounds. On Harbord, the top of what was once the Harbord Bridge peeks out of the ground. At Montrose and Beatrice, you wouldn't know it, but the public school's playground offers a sign that tells us we're standing at the Garrison Creek Ravine. It goes on.

Though Garrison Creek may have disappeared beneath our feet long ago, it isn't entirely gone yet. Local groups have walking tours that follow the course of "lost rivers" like Garrison Creek, while others are pushing the city to restore the ravine systems and help its inhabitants rediscover the green history of their own communities.

live outside walking distance from the commercial centre of Toronto, and a correspondingly large demand for big houses on sprawling picturesque lots. Though it might have been the time of the first railway schemes, civic boosterism, the end of the waterfront as a pleasure promenade (sold off to the railway companies) and the beginning of Toronto's challenge to the commercial dominance of Montreal, almost all the land north of Queen and west of the university (to the city limits of Dufferin and Bloor) remained in the hands of "old" families: Baldwin, Denison, Crookshank and Givens. These old-money park-lot owners and their heirs prepared for civic growth and potentially outsized profits in the parcelling out of their land for more rich people.

But the boom did not come quickly, nor did it reach expectations. A detailed atlas of the city in 1858 showed those holdings to be a mostly empty quarter, dissected by deep ravines, and bird's-eye views in the late 1870s showed the same rustic landscape.

By now, the urban growth of Toronto, as the provincial capital in a new Canada, began to pick up serious momentum, but in a different social direction than before. Toronto became more industrial than mercantile, and more of a regional centre than one town among many. A brief spurt of immigration after Confederation, coupled with the beginnings of larger-scale industrialization in the new Canada, led to accelerated demand for new housing for rapidly developing working and middle classes. This meant houses on small lots rather than the colonial country estates of the merchant

elite. Rosedale, the Annex and other posh estates were lined up to capture the market for big urban mansions on relatively small lots. Large-scale property speculation turned toward the production of large tracts of far more modest dwellings at the edges of town, enabled by the imminent extension of the newfangled technology of the streetcar.

Now there was a lot more money to be made in planting houses on their picturesque lands rather than pasture and vegetables.

Most of the "empty" northwest quarter belonged to several generations of the Denison family, surrounding three genteel but declining country estates — Dover Court, Rusholme and Heydon Villa. Chunks of their southern frontages along Dundas and Queen had been sold off as big house lots to generate cash for George T. Denison's heirs, and the names of the several Denisons were joined by newer wealth on the property rolls, such as Bickford, Shaw and Crawford. Soon enough these "newcomers" started to divide up their own lots.

As land ownership began to fragment further, access to new lots from the older public streets to the south became progressively constrained, persuading the owners in the northern parts of the western park lots to consider very seriously an eastern connection past the university lands toward Yonge Street.

In 1873, the architect and surveyor John Howard donated to the city a vast tract that would become High Park. Almost immediately, the Denisons and their friends proposed that

Building Garrison Creek sewer (circa 1890s). Photo: TA

Sully Crescent near College Street. Photographer William James's note on the photograph reads: "To be filled up to the bridge, Crawford and Shaw Streets will then be level without bridges. 50 houses will be vacated." (1911). Photo: TA

Sully Crescent and its bordering houses, before the ravine was filled in (1907). Photo: TA

LEFT: Palmerston Avenue looking south from Harbord when it was a new suburb (1908). Photo: TA. RIGHT: Palmerston looking south from Harbord today. Photo: Bryan Gee

the city create a "driving park" through their empty lands: really, a westward extension of College Street to the new public park.

There was, however, a problem: the dead end of College at Manning Avenue. J.M. Strachan's 1846 subdivision of the "Crookshank Block" (a narrow strip from Queen to Bloor centred on Clinton Street) had blocked the westward extension of College for three decades. The current owner of the strategic blocks, one William Wakefield, was apparently holding out for a fair (that is, fairly high) "urban" price for the small section of pasture required to extend the street west. City Council, not wishing to extend itself unduly for land speculators, had simply let the matter die in committee (the Board of Works), and there it sat for five years.

But the city's growth became relentless, and rapid colonization of its empty northwest was only a matter of time. By 1879, there was street railway under construction on College between Spadina and Bathurst, and the city engineer apparently now thought well enough of the idea of extending College westward to convince Council to appropriate $2,000 toward the extension of the street. The western landowners, exhilarated at the prospect of opening their lands to access not only by street, but by streetcar as well, offered a rare demonstration of co-operative speculation, and laid out a westward extension of College straight through their holdings in the hope that the city would buy the street allowance and extend the streetcar line – all the way to High Park.

This time the municipal authorities began to oblige rather quickly.

Unhappily, despite the urgings of its more progressive citizens (at least as represented in the Toronto *Globe*), the width of the new College Street extension was not the 99- or 100-foot boulevard or driving park of Baldwin's original urban vision, but rather the standard 66-foot Toronto street allowance. Sixty-six feet was good enough for a main street with streetcar everywhere else and, besides, the extra cost wasn't worth the "lost" property taxes from a few lots. The penny-pinching Council bought just the minimum street, and let the speculators and subdividers do what they would with the rest.

On paper, all was now fine. But the real terrain was less forgiving. Though not quite the equivalent of the Don River to the east, the valleys of Garrison Creek and its tributary Brewery Creek were more than just part of the country charm of the old estates. They were physical barriers to construction of roads, services and houses. To extend College straight west would plunge it into a deep and flood-prone ravine right out to the city limits at Dufferin, too steep for both buildings and streetcars.

To resolve the problem, surveyors drew up a crescent in 1879 that would sidestep the ravine by going northwestward.

But the alignment on paper worked very poorly on the ground, and in 1885, Council took the very unusual step of moving the "wiggle" to a narrower part of the ravine,

reducing the amount of landfill and better accommodating the speed of an electrified streetcar. Of course, since the new street on higher ground took up more of their buildable lots than did the ravine route, the speculators demanded extra compensation for the realignment, not just swaps of land. In addition, the city was forced to remove at least one new house that could have been built only months before.

Further west, Charles Lindsey had acquired a portion of an old estate lot and found, no doubt to his dismay, that the edge of the oncoming College Street would be barely 70 feet away from the southern limit of his parcel, insufficient for marketable building lots on both sides of the new thoroughfare. Accordingly, he demanded that his piece of the extension of College be moved further north, with an inevitable kink at what is now Havelock. The city had little choice but to agree with the landowner.

Toronto's western city limits had been set at Dufferin Street in 1834, and although this northwest frontier was still mostly empty of buildings, the city began a 30-year program of territorial expansion in 1883, with new streetcar lines quick to follow. College Street was extended from Dufferin west through the former village of Brockton in 1886. An extension to what is now Lansdowne was approved the next year, and by 1890 the first few houses began to appear. College even appeared on ambitious subdivision plans all the way west to High Park, but the crucial connection across the railroad tracks that led to Toronto Junction was never made.

College and Bay, southwest corner (1890). Photo: TPL

College and Spadina, northwest corner (1870). Photo: TPL

LEFT: South side of College between University and Elizabeth (1907). Photo: TPL

What would have been College Street became Grenadier Avenue.

But it was the installation of the streetcar that really defined College at the end of the 19th century. The College car line reached Dufferin in 1889 and High Park (via Dundas and Howard Park Avenue) in 1893. By then, the line was all electric, with faster and more frequent service that dramatically extended the practicable commuting distance to downtown. The proposed operation of this one route on Sundays became an epic political struggle of old Protestant Tory Toronto to hang on to its Victorian rectitude and propriety against those who would weaken the Christian Sabbath. In order to give city residents summertime access to the recreation grounds

of High Park, a fierce battle in the press and City Council began in 1888, and the dust did not settle on the question until 1897, and only after a full civic plebiscite had finally approved Sunday operation.

At the end of the 19th century, almost all of College had been subdivided into building lots. Much of the land north and south was filling up rapidly with new houses. Yet very little of the street's actual frontage west of the ravines had any buildings yet. For that matter, there even remained empty frontages around Bathurst Street. College had not been so much pushed out from the city, by pressures to build the city out along its commercial thoroughfares, as it had been pulled out into the countryside, as a route to the

extensive suburban tracts under development on either side, and to the one big piece of parkland available to anyone for the price of a streetcar ticket. Many blocks of College Street remained empty at the end of the 19th century, waiting for their values to be pushed up by 20th-century ambition and speculation.

... and how to grow it

For many years after the actual completion of the street, the most conspicuous constructions on College were the billboards.

Property speculation, a constant preoccupation of 21st-century Toronto, is as old as the city's first house lot in

54

Billboards on the south side of College Street, just east of Bathurst (circa 1910s). Photo: TA

An accident on the road forces the T.R. Car No. 531 to stop on College just west of Brock Avenue (Sept. 10, 1915). Photo: TA

College and Spadina (Sept. 14, 1925). Photo: TA

1793. What really energized the speculation and the eventual development of College Street was the streetcar, and the accompanying promise of higher land values, bigger buildings and crowded sidewalks full of workers and shoppers. For some parts of the street, through various periods of the 20th century, that promise of development was fulfilled, but in a syncopated, mixed and ultimately very interesting way – not quite as everyone might have imagined. As a result, some sections have buildings that survive as grand expressions of architectural ambition in different periods, others play more modest supporting roles and a few don't co-operate very well at all.

Earlier arterial extensions of the city's commercial core along Yonge, King and Queen had consisted of built-up frontages concealing relatively less dense, even undeveloped, zones behind. But when the electric streetcar began to replace the horse car in the 1880s, the old approach to city building sped up and began to turn inside out.

College and the other newer streetcar strips were commercial and institutional service spines not only for the recent neighbourhoods immediately behind, but also for the newer and somewhat wealthier middle-class neighbourhoods further out, districts that were being built up at roughly the same time as the streetcar strip itself. There might have been an older house here and there in the western reaches of College Street, and a few early mixed-use walk-ups with apartments above stores, but the frontages were filled in seriously only afterwards, once the outlying residential districts served by the strip's streetcar line were being filled in themselves. Residential neighbourhoods north and south of College out to Lansdowne were almost completely built up and occupied between 1900 and 1910. But College's own frontages before 1910 were barely half-filled. Much of the remainder was constructed in a huge building boom just before the 1914 World War, just as the newest middle-class suburbs were filling up further west at High Park.

Of course, the boom times on these newer strips would end when retail commerce arrived in those outer suburbs (along Roncesvalles, and Bloor west of High Park). The added

55

CONTINUED PAGE 58

The Perfect Streetcar Strip

Since streetcars first began running on College, the tracks have periodically required repair and replacement, giving work to road crews, while interrupting business for local merchants. These tracks were laid in 1936.

BELOW: College looking west from Grace.
OPPOSITE PAGE TOP: College looking west from Clinton.
OPPOSITE PAGE BOTTOM: College looking east from Grace.
Photos: TA

retail competition to the west took the steam out of development on College. It was all a matter of timing. That meant there were still empty frontages on College Street – great swaths of billboards, actually – when everything around those lots had been built and occupied decades before. Some owners caught the biggest wave, others managed to get by and others still missed it altogether – with some faint hope that another wave of development would pay off later on. Some College frontages from the 1920s sit in front of housing finished off in the 1890s.

The result: a perfect street for the 20th century
The building type most characteristic of College Street is the walk-up, a combination of residence above and commerce on the sidewalk. Most walk-ups on College are retail stores (including restaurants, bars and any other kind of place to spend money) with residences above, usually one or two flats, or occasionally a small apartment building. The mixed-use walk-up was a "traditional" downtown or small-town building type that is very rarely built today, and even then only on streets where they already exist. (Toronto has always preferred its residences to be owner-occupied houses with gardens, and anything else – even the most expensive penthouse condo – still bears a stigma.)

With the introduction of more and more inflexible zoning and building regulations since the middle of the 20th century, residences seldom appear mixed in with other uses in the city. There are minor exceptions, mostly in the very centre of the city, but most of today's Toronto, whether smaller or "greater," is quite different from the urban and suburban landscapes of yesterday for one very simple reason: no mixing allowed.

Why this is so has many rather confused explanations, but the general idea is that city property is worth more where different uses and activities are separated from each other. And, according to conventional wisdom, it's not that cities make property valuable, but rather it's property value that makes cities. Conventional wisdom loves real estate.

Given Toronto's traditional preference for owner-occupied

College and Euclid, today. Photo: Mark Fram (detail)

houses, commercial walk-ups were rarely continuous on College and other strips. Retail commerce has a long and well-known history of high failure rates. For owners who wanted a long-term income from property rents, as well as the chance for bigger returns when the time was right, the walk-up provided a bit of both. Speculators, on the other hand, might leave their properties vacant instead, hoping for a much bigger future profit from the conditions established by earlier bidders.

Even today, as you go further west, there is a mix of regular detached or semi-detached houses next to storefronts built out in front of those same houses, and alongside walk-ups whose ground floors don't have shops. There are a few

"archaeological" rooflines of original houses poking up behind old shopfronts.

The walk-ups on College appeared during three principal surges of construction that follow the peaks of residential building cycles in Toronto. The number of retail addresses on the street increased most rapidly a year or two after the peaks of Toronto building booms in 1889, 1911 and 1922. New shops appeared to cater to the arrival of the new inhabitants, and those arrivals lagged behind the house completions.

But even once built, retail buildings were especially sensitive to subsequent business cycles. Optimistic overbuilding during booms led to high vacancy rates for years afterwards, and between peaks, commercial building virtually ceased.

In the case of the great depression of the 1890s, there was almost no building of any kind, though during the First World War other construction did go on at a reduced pace. The peak years of the 1920s almost filled up the last available vacant lots on College and then began to replace older buildings. These replacements, as well as the move toward larger residential-only apartment buildings, did not produce much new commerce on the more western frontages of College after the 1920s. By 1930, College Street was no longer the edge of town. Some of its storefronts were never filled.

The long, syncopated stretches of dwellings and shops are further punctuated by churches, schools and institutions, but apart from the oldest of them all, St. Stephen's at

Bellevue Avenue (constructed by the Denison family almost as their own chapel), each of these developments had to acquire its lands in the rather rough property market after everything had been subdivided. Churches, schools and parks might enable a certain respectability of tone and image (what we now call quality of life), but they weren't as lucrative to the land market as were houses, offices and factories. Nevertheless, through a wide range of religious denominations, fraternal organizations and (eventually) civic agencies, the street eventually filled in its places of worship, assembly, play and education. And, curiously enough, for a part of the city already surrounded by houses with no railway tracks, even a few factories – though nowadays many have become "lofts," remade for conspicuous consumption rather than everyday production.

The stores and bars and cafés that now line the street offer a wide variety of settings for smaller-scale shifts of form. There remain huge plate-glass displays of merchandise alongside identical fronts papered over with flyers for long-distance cards and lotteries. There are still glazed transoms over tall doorways, right next to big fluorescent sign boxes covering up everything. Some canvas awnings still protect store windows and entrances. Original recessed entries allow the window-shopper halfway into the store before opening the door. Neighbouring bars with garage doors at the sidewalk join outside to inside in good weather and become a double-entry threshold for evicted cigarette smokers.

But up above, apart from some cheap sliding windows and the disappearance of some original architectural ornament (to be reattached one day, perhaps?), the century-old walls

that line the street are mostly intact. Bit by bit – just as in the past – the street is changing with its times.

What you see ...

The eastern end of the street – originally a collection of old houses, factories, warehouses and slum dwellings that became Eaton's College Street store, and now the development called College Park – is simply the grandest example of architectural ambition on College Street, as much for what didn't happen there as for what did. The seven-storey block at the corner of Yonge was intended at its commencement in 1928 to be merely part of the base for a 50-something-storey complex – until economic depression stopped the dream. Or, as it has turned out, only delayed it, since the newest residential towers are pretty much the height planned in the 1920s.

College Street walk-ups, today. Photos: Mark Fram

For the next several blocks to the west, the street is a mix of institutions and flash: the MaRS complex, the Toronto General Hospital, the medical and engineering buildings of the University of Toronto, glazed chunks of provincial government agencies, lumpy intrusions by the university into the public street. The further west you go, the more muted become the grand scale and sanitary frontages until the first of the street's kinks, at Spadina. Which is where College Street becomes the familiar and mixed-up terrain you now know all about.

And where the street becomes *much* more interesting.

West of Spadina, College Street was cobbled together from bits and pieces over the last half of the 19th century. While it was all there out to Lansdowne by 1893, and its immediate neighbourhoods were filling in rapidly, the actual walls that line the street today took several decades to appear. College was a paved road for bicycles, horse-drawn vans and street-cars long before the private automobile arrived. But the early subdivision of most of the streets into house lots ensured that ongoing development would have to remain pretty small for the most part, thus preserving – to the chagrin of city planners, "modern" property developers and big institutions – that new development would happen along the street in minor increments and syncopated tempo. Vacant lots, construction sites and billboards were just as much part of the early streetcar views as were new houses, churches and walk-ups.

College is really a fricassee of time and style, and its variety and vitality remain distinctive in its building facades, on its crowded sidewalks and at its corner cafés. If there's a method to its distinction, it's that for the most part only small bits of the street are able to change at any one time, and even then, the neighbours are still there to keep watch.

And so College Street thrives – arguably better than any other street – as Toronto's definitive streetcar strip and pedestrian promenade.

BILLIARDS
CIGARS
IGARETTES

Smoke
Ogden's
Cut Plug

Smoke
Ogd

The Jewish Experience

From College to Cullij and Back

RICHARD MENKIS & HAROLD TROPER

For five decades, College Street was a core artery for the many Toronto Jews who set down roots in the surrounding neighbourhoods. But these roots also twist back to the Russian Pale of Settlement in the 1880s. Jews had lived for centuries in this western reach of a slowly decaying Tsarist empire, a region that today includes much of Poland, Lithuania, Ukraine and Belarus. During the last quarter of the 19th century, the Jews in the Pale were subjected to repressive and hostile anti-Jewish legislation. The Tsarist government also instigated a series of pogroms that killed, maimed and further impoverished a Jewish population already hobbled by surging numbers and a corrosive economic decline in the smaller towns and villages that were home to many Jews. Desperate to escape violence or simply to feed a family, tens of thousands of Jews fled rural areas of the Pale into larger and more urban industrial centres. Still others escaped the Pale entirely, pushing westward into western Europe and Britain. But for many, the destination was still further west – the new world. From the 1880s through to the outbreak of the First World War in 1914, Jews formed a major part of the larger exodus of eastern and southern European immigrants then streaming out of European ports toward the Western Hemisphere.

This surge of immigration out of Europe proved fortuitous for Canada. At the turn of the 20th century, as many immigrants set off to build a new life in a new land, Canada was ushering in an unprecedented era of economic expansion. Driving the new prosperity was a sharp increase in international markets for metals and lumber from newly accessible regions of the Canadian Shield and western mountain regions. There was also an insatiable demand for grains from the vast and still underpopulated Canadian prairies that was opened to settlement with the completion of the Canadian Pacific Railway. To feed this international market, Canada sought workers to meet the needs of labour-intensive resource industries and farmers to work the lands of western Canada. Rather than just hope immigrants would choose to come to Canada, the Canadian government initiated major immigrant recruitment in Europe designed to divert the outflow of European immigrants toward Canada. The government succeeded. Eastern European immigrants settled the vast expanse of western farmland or found work in the mines, forests and mills of the Canadian hinterland.

The prosperity fed by the surging agricultural and raw material exports also created prosperity in Canadian urban centres (which witnessed a boom in construction), modernization of the urban infrastructure and a rapid expansion in secondary manufacturing and service industries. Toronto was no exception. The city grew quickly, and immigrants, including Jews, filled many of the unskilled, semi-skilled and craft jobs in the expanded service and manufacturing industries. In 1903, there were only 3,100 Jews in Toronto. The majority were of an early generation of well-integrated Anglo-Jewish merchant shopkeepers and those in the wholesale import and export business. As a result of immigration, by 1931, the number of Jews in Toronto had increased fifteenfold and hovered close to 50,000. Through the end of the Second World War, Jews were both the largest immigrant community in Toronto as well as Toronto's largest non-Christian community.

Many of the new Jewish arrivals – desperately poor, Yiddish-speaking and unschooled in the ways of a Canadian city – found themselves relegated to St. John's Ward (often simply called the Ward). It was a neighbourhood with arguably the worst housing in the city, but with ready access to nearby employment and public transit. But this down-on-its-heels, immigrant-receiving neighbourhood was not invisible to the larger community. It couldn't be. It was in the very centre of the city. The densely populated Ward was bordered on the east by Yonge Street and on the west by University Avenue, on the south by Queen Street and on the north by College Street. If a line were drawn connecting Toronto's City Hall at Queen and Bay with the Ontario Parliament buildings at the foot of Queen's Park just north of College Street, that line would almost exactly bisect the Ward.

The Jews who made up the majority of those in the Ward lived cheek-by-jowl with other recent arrivals, particularly Italians, in one- and two-storey low-rent houses, often tiny shack-like frame or rough-cast structures subdivided to house several families. Many of these immigrants found wage labour in the Eaton's clothing factory or with other ready-for-the-rack clothing manufacturers that hovered along the southern and western fringe of the Ward. But some immigrants sidestepped the *shmatte* (literally "rags,"

OPPOSITE: Louis Starkman Billiard Parlour, 355 College, circa 1930. Photo: JA

but colloquially referring to clothing) industry. Risk takers and those confident in their entrepreneurial skills tried their hands in businesses – often as peddlers, jobbers, small shopkeepers. Some limited their economic horizons to serving the market needs of the surrounding Jewish community, while others eyed the larger client market of a growing Toronto.

But whether salaried workers or struggling merchants, the Jews of the Ward avoided College Street to their north. On Dundas and Queen to the south, they found streets wide open to immigrant commercial enterprise and amenable to Jewish social interaction. Not so with College. To the Jews, the buildings that lined either side of College Street immediately north of the Ward did not just represent the northern border of the Ward. They also represented a stolid mortar-and-brick-walled fortress of Anglo-Protestant institutions, cold to the immigrant touch. On the south side of College Street, in the first block west from Yonge to what is now Bay Street, stood Bishop Strachan School, a private Anglican girls' school founded in 1867, the year of Confederation. In 1915, the school was converted into a veterans hospital to care for the war wounded. Moving west, at College and Elizabeth was the Hospital for Sick Children. Many Jews knew this building well – as outsiders. Affixed to a side entrance to the children's hospital, a few steps down from College, a black-and-white painted sign in English, Italian and Yiddish announced that this door, not the imposing hospital front door on College, was the entrance to a clinic for the local

poor. West across Elizabeth and stretching along College all the way to University Avenue was the site of Toronto General Hospital, off limits to Jewish doctors whether on staff, as interns or as residents.

The north side of College was just as inhospitably remote to the immigrant Jews of the Ward. Hugging the northern corner of College at Yonge was a red-brick office building filled with doctors' and dentists' offices, with not one recognizable Jewish name among them. A few doors west stood another office building, home to the Canadian Bible Society organized in 1905 and whose members, Bibles at the ready, pledged to spread Christ's message to the heathen. And who were the closest heathen but the growing Jewish community

at the organization's doorstep. Only a few doors west from the Canadian Bible Society was the Forester Building, which housed the Girl Guides of Canada and a Christian Science Reading Room. Close by was the YMCA – the Young Men's Christian Association – then preaching a vision of muscular Christianity and offering Christian-infused social service outreach to the community. In the next block westward, between Elizabeth and University, was the Zion Congregational Church and the evangelical Toronto Bible College. Just north up University Avenue from the corner of College were the imposing red sandstone Provincial Parliament Buildings, seat of government in Ontario. The men of political power and social influence who ruled Ontario from their perch

Markham Street. The stones were for people to step up into their carriages. Photo: TA

overlooking College Street, barely a five-minute walk from the gritty shanty world of the Ward, might just as well have been a million miles away for what little they shared in common with their immigrant Jewish neighbours to the south. This was equally so for the elite, ivory-towered University of Toronto, fanning out westward beyond Queen's Park north of College.

If working-class immigrant Jews regarded College Street immediately to their north as an uninviting bastion of Anglo-Protestant Toronto before the First World War, the same was not true of interwar College Street west from McCaul Street past Spadina Avenue to Bathurst Street and eventually all the way to Ossington Avenue. In the years following the First

World War, this stretch of College Street replaced the Ward as the centre of Jewish community life in Toronto. What became of the Ward? The Jewish population of the Ward was displaced by urban reformers and area landlords. In the years before the First World War, the fact of a squalid and crowded immigrant neighbourhood – in the very shadow of City Hall's bell tower – was increasingly condemned by urban reformers as a social blight and an unsanitary threat to public health. They demanded the whole area be razed to the ground. This was music to the ears of landowners, speculators and developers who relished the prospect of massive and profitable redevelopment, not of the area's existing rental stock, but of new commercial and business construction.

As city fathers, reformers and developers talked up the benefits of urban renewal, rising property values pushed rents up and Jews out of the Ward. It is unlikely that many of those Jews pushed out of St. John's Ward much regretted packing up and leaving. The Ward was no Eden. The issue was not whether to go, but where to go. For most, the answer was obvious. Jews from the Ward, joined by new immigrants arriving daily in Toronto, shifted westward. So did much of the clothing manufacturing industry, the mainstay of Jewish employment, which relocated into newly built multi-level factories on lower Spadina Avenue. The Ward now to their back and the *shmatte* trade nearby, Jews moved into two- and three-storey low-rent properties that dominated the side

Talmud Torah and YMHA on Brunswick Avenue (1950), Photo: JA

Brunswick Talmud Torah graduating class. Photo: OA

Outside Benny Rotenberg's store, 566 College (1930s). Photo courtesy of Fäggie Rotenberg Oliver

streets that ran north and south off College or parallel to it. The intersection of College and Spadina was soon the city's major Jewish intersection – the Times Square of Toronto Jewry. This Jewish infill remade the surrounding neighbourhood. In 1901, the streets west of Spadina that intersected College from the Kensington Market area to the north and south were as much as 80 per cent Anglo-Canadian. Year by year that changed, until by the mid-1920s these same streets were home to a majority Jewish population with College Street as its central east-west artery.

College, rolling westward from Spadina, became the well-trod and vibrant Jewish community corridor with a character – some might even say charm – all its own and certainly very different from the other major arteries that transected the Toronto Jewish neighbourhood. Queen Street and Dundas Avenue to the south remained streets of core Jewish commerce and business, both wholesale and retail. Many of these businesses – jobbers, sewing-machine repair shops, thread and button wholesalers, and even lunch-counter restaurants – were dependent on the nearby *shmatte* trade. Others sold ready-to-wear men's and ladies' clothing to the public, perhaps trying to skim bargain-hunting customers away from the Eaton's and Simpson's department stores only a few blocks away. Kensington Market, a little further northwest, had a lock on food merchandising and, as Jewish numbers in the area increased, it soon dominated the kosher-food business as well. Kosher butcher shops with live poultry in cages or fish stores with carp, white fish and pike swimming

in large tanks and soon to be ground up for *gefilte fish*, were located next to fruit and vegetable stores or bakeries specializing in the hard-crusted breads, bagels and egg-loaf challahs that eastern Europe Jews favoured.

And what of College Street? College Street did not compete against the business and commercial areas of Dundas and Queen, nor did it siphon off the food-related enterprise dominated by Kensington Market. No, College was different. It was primarily a street of social interaction and a street that addressed the day-to-day needs of Jewish families who lived within a few minutes' walk. And College Street pulsed with Jewish community life. Walking west along College from Spadina, all the way to Ossington, shoppers passed one Jewish-owned business after another. There were a number of Jewish tailor shops where skilled craftsmen cut and sold custom-made suits as opposed to the off-the-rack items then available from Tip Top Tailors, on the northeast corner of College and Spadina, or the many ready-to-wear stores further south on Spadina. Of course, there was nothing the matter with an off-the-rack suit, but for those who were "doing well" and those who were a little more style-conscious, why not have a business suit or a son's bar mitzvah suit or a wife's dress for the High Holidays made to measure?

Rich and poor still rubbed shoulders in the confectionaries, drugstores, photographers' shops, shoe stores, barber shops, hardware stores and dairies that lined the street. On College one could buy a Yiddish newspaper – whether Toronto's own daily, the *Yiddisher Zhurnal*, or for the more

radical reader, *Der Veg*, or one of the competing Yiddish papers from New York – almost as readily as one of the city's major English-language dailies. And why not read the paper in one of the local delicatessens, where animated patrons solved the problems of the world while downing thick corned beef sandwiches on rye with mustard, coleslaw and a pickle? The topic of discussion might be a little earthier, but no less animated, in any one of the several pool halls along College. Out front of a pool hall any warm summer night, one was likely to find a group of young men just hanging out and eyeing the girls walking by, while chewing on *shemishkes*, sunflower and pumpkin seeds. After several hours, the sidewalk was carpeted with shells. And reflecting the gradual emergence of a new university-educated Jewish middle class, College Street proved fertile ground for Jewish professionals looking for a core clientele. At least two Jewish dentists opened up offices on College, as did a Jewish optometrist. Jewish lawyers, knowing they would never be able to join the larger Anglo law firms in downtown Toronto, rented office space above local stores and built their practices.

For these shopkeepers and professionals, as well as for their customers and clients, College Street was home turf. Everyone seemed to live nearby. The web of streets that ran north and south off College, or parallel to it, was home to tens of thousands of Yiddish-speaking immigrants and their Canadian-born children. The Jewish map of the College Street area was inclusive of Major, Brunswick, Borden, Lippincott, Markham, Palmerston, Euclid, Manning, Ulster,

Interior of Benny Rotenberg's store, 566 College (1930s). Photo courtesy of Fäggie Rotenberg Oliver

Masthead of the *Daily Hebrew Journal*, or *Yiddisher Zhurnal*, from Feb. 7, 1969. Photo: JA

Augusta, Bellevue, Oxford and Nassau, all streets named to honour Toronto's British imperial heritage. But to the many Jews who lived on these streets during the interwar years, these names might just as well have been in Yiddish, and in many cases they sounded as if they were. It might take a streetcar conductor a while to decipher a request for information on when to get off the *Cullij* line at *Majeh*, *Brunzvik*, *Bordin*, *Pulmest'n*, *Meningk*, *Ulsteh* or *Nesah*.

But everyone, including the streetcar conductor on the College Street line, knew that *Cullij Strit* had a special *tam*, a special flavour all its own. Certainly, *Cullij Strit* was Toronto's busy central Jewish artery. But it was more than that. It was also a very human street that mirrored the day-to-day life of the surrounding Jewish community. On College, neighbour met neighbour. There always seemed time to gossip, talk politics, brag about a child's success, complain about back pain, debate the merits of one rabbi over another, lament the high cost and low quality of local produce and offer advice – solicited or not. To quote boxer Sammy Luftspring, "For us Jews, the world of College and Spadina never stopped buzzing."

But if College Street pulsed with Jewish activity, it also both separated Jews from the rest of the city and separated Jew from Jew by class. For the more financially successful Jewish merchants, professionals and even shop owners, several streets that ran north from College – particularly Markham and Palmerston – offered larger, finer properties to rent and, increasingly, to buy. Just knowing that someone lived on Palmerston north of College rather than south of College was enough to suggest a class boundary had been crossed. Here was someone obviously not chained to a sewing machine on Spadina. Here was someone on a trajectory of upward mobility.

Oddly, however, for all the street life on College, there were few Jewish communal institutions and organizations to be found on the street itself. For example, no synagogues were housed on College Street. The left-wing Zionist Borochov School was one of the few exceptions, operating in the interwar years. Why the general absence of organizational activity on this busy Jewish street? It's hard to know. Perhaps rent-per-foot or the cost of land for those organizations seeking to own their own building was prohibitively high on College Street. In any event, synagogues and Jewish institutions were most often located on the off-streets, even if only a few minutes walk from College. The Romanian Synagogue, for example, was on Bathurst just north of College. And in an often fractious Jewish community, synagogues and organizations abounded and reflected virtually every shade of thought – religiously observant or secular, politically right, centre, left or still further left; Zionist, non-Zionist and anti-Zionist; Yiddishist, Hebraist or English speaking. There was a place for the boss and the worker, the artist and the shopkeeper, the dreamer and the pragmatist, the scholar and the athlete. Synagogues shared city blocks with union halls and offices of *landsmanshaft* – mutual benefit societies grounded in their members' common place of origin in eastern Europe. In a Toronto before universal public unemployment insurance and medicare, for those in unionized sections of the garment industry, it was either membership in a *landsmanshaft* or a union that guaranteed access to a doctor on retainer and assistance in the case of injury. In the event of death, a prepaid burial plot with all the appropriate religious rites – if desired – was assured; the bereaved widow or orphans would not be abandoned without care.

In addition to these grass-roots organizations, the Jewish community gradually organized a range of organizations and institutions to support and serve a broader segment of the community that straddled College Street. Among the more prominent of these were the Brunswick Talmud Torah, the Young Men's Hebrew Association (YMHA) and the Jewish Immigrant Aid Service. In 1925, the Brunswick Talmud Torah, a Jewish day school, proudly opened the doors to its new building on Brunswick just north of College. While the vast majority of Jewish children attended local public schools, the Talmud Torah offered the community a Jewish alternative, a school modern in approach that offered students both a traditional Jewish education as well as a full program of secular subjects. To the school's detractors, it seemed a little too modern, a little too ready to adapt to Canadian ways. To its defenders, however, the school was a symbol of Jews adapting to Canada without losing their attachment to tradition. It also seemed to promise a rare Jewish unity when a Reform rabbi joined two Orthodox rabbis at the opening ceremonies.

Sammy Luftspring

One-time Canadian welterweight champion Sammy Luftspring in his memoirs recalled the College and Spadina of the '20s, the intersection "never stopped buzzing" with restaurants and social gathering places. At the Standard Theatre, his parents would sneak in the young Sammy at intermissions. This was, in Luftspring's words, "my first wide-eyed exposure to the thrills of having an audience, and incidentally my first taste of that audience-hunger, which has stuck with me all my life."

To Luftspring, growing up in the slum environment of Baldwin and Kensington proved to be his early training, whereby differences were settled with physical force. Most of his opponents shared the same background of young men of ghettos, whether they were Jews, Italians, Irish or Slavic.

Sammy was selected for the 1936 Munich Olympic team representing Canada, but his parents later convinced the boxer to boycott the games. A joint statement with teammate boxer Norman "Baby" Yack stated: "[C]an Canadian sportsmen blame us for refusing to take part in a meet sponsored by people who would humiliate and degrade and persecute us too if we did not have the great fortune of being Canadians?"

By 1938, Luftspring, fighting as a professional, had attained the Canadian welterweight title by felling Frankie Genovese in a 15-round match. Luftspring's ascent in the profession would be short-lived as a combatant; an errant punch and thumb in Luftspring's eye would blind the fighter on one side, retiring Luftspring the boxer at 24. Eventually Luftspring would return to the ring as a referee for over 2,000 matches, while also operating two downtown nightclubs, the Mercury on Victoria Street and the Brown Derby at Dundas and Yonge.

A New York advertisement featuring local boxer, Sammy Luftspring, Welterweight Champion of Canada. Photo: JA

LEFT: Sammy Luftspring, Harry Sniderman and Norman "Baby" Yack aboard the SS Alavnia bound for Barcelona (July 11, 1936). Photo: JA

"FOR EVERY ROUND OF THE DAY, I WEAR AN ADAM HAT"

SAMMY LUFTSPRING

WELTERWEIGHT CHAMPION OF CANADA

COSMOPOLITAN N·Y·

Nathan Phillips

"In plain language, I will try and be you, all the people of Toronto." Nathan Phillips's diverse appeal and eventual distinction as the "Mayor of All the People" arose out of his 36 years of service to the people of Toronto. He spent eight of these years as the city's longest serving mayor, not to mention its first of Jewish background.

Before Phillips became mayor, he was Ward 4's representative on City Council for 28 years. Initially elected in 1924, the Osgoode Hall Law School-trained lawyer Phillips became Toronto's youngest alderman.

Phillips originally had an eye toward a provincial or federal office, thinking to run in his riding as a Conservative candidate. But he stayed on as his ward's alderman. And then came an event that would launch Phillips into his mayoral destiny.

Just before the municipal elections, with Phillips contesting for mayor, then-incumbent mayor Leslie Saunders set off a pre-election controversy that would effectively send Phillips to the mayor's office. Saunders had made some ill-advised comments at the ceremony of the Glorious Twelfth, the annual Toronto Orangemen parade to the Exhibition Grounds, as well as publishing a list of voting recommendations listing candidates' religious and political affiliations. Local newspapers jumped on Saunders' actions immediately.

When Phillips eventually won the election, he said in his victory speech, "I cannot help but mention the sour note thrown into the campaign by one of the opponents which emphasized the fact that I am of the Jewish faith with the clear object of defeating me." He thanked the city's voters for rejecting Saunders' smear campaign and said that he would represent "all the people in the broadest sense."

Murray Koffler, the founder of Shoppers Drug Mart, as a child with his aunt in front of his father's store, Koffler's Drugs, at 376 College (1927). Photo: JA

Schools were not the only institutions that served Jewish children. In the years after the First World War, there was growing Jewish community concern that Jewish children left to play unsupervised in the street after school could get into trouble, but, if allowed to participate in programs organized outside the Jewish community – including those of the local YMCA, only minutes east along College near Yonge Street – they could be subject to unwelcome Christian proselytization. To afford a Jewish option, the YMHA was founded, and fundraising to build a modest athletic facility, including a gymnasium and a swimming pool, began. As it happened, the Talmud Torah was also looking for an athletic facility. After some negotiation, a deal was struck. Sharing costs and facilities, the YMHA was built adjacent to the school. The school used the gym during the school day, and the "Y," which was also charged with administering the athletic wing, used it at all other times. The YMHA building on Brunswick, just north of College, was more than the sum of its parts – it had become a community centre.

The YMHA's facilities were well-used in the immigrant Jewish community. One of Jewish Toronto's favourite sons was the talented boxer Sammy Luftspring. A local kid who first boxed at the YMHA, Luftspring frequently wore a Star of David on his boxing trunks. Regarded as a hero in the College Street neighbourhood, Luftspring was selected for the 1936 Canadian Olympic team. But he and another Toronto Jewish boxer, Norman "Baby" Yack, created a stir when they announced they would boycott the games scheduled for

Toronto Jewish Community Softball League (1929). Photo: AO

OPENING OF JEWISH COMMUNITY SOFTBALL LEAGUE, TORONTO, MAY 7, 1929.

Berlin in protest against Nazi persecution of Jews and other minority groups. Luftspring turned professional later on, but never completely realized his potential after suffering a debilitating eye injury.

Like the YMHA, the Jewish Immigrant Aid Society (JIAS) was founded shortly after the First World War. It was originally organized to assist in the settlement of post-war Jewish immigrants and to help Jews already in Toronto apply to bring family and friends to Canada. But its role was about to change, just as it was opening its office on the southeast corner of Spadina and College. In response to growing anti-immigrant sentiment and declining demand for immigrant labour, the Canadian government imposed draconian immigration restrictions that cut deeply into the flow of immigration from southern and eastern Europe, particularly Jewish immigration. During the 1930s, as economic hardship and the horror of Fascism and Nazism fell over European Jewry, their growing desperation was mirrored in the faces of Jews on College Street. Desperate to bring threatened family from Europe to Canada, Jews lined up at the JIAS office to fill out immigration applications on behalf of family in Europe, but almost always for naught. Canada and Canadians were unmoved by the plight of European Jewry – or not moved enough to open Canada's doors. With Jews excluded from Canada, many of the Jewish households in the College Street neighbourhood would soon grieve the loss of brothers and sisters, mothers and fathers, in the systematic mass murder of the Holocaust.

But if the outbreak of war against Germany in September 1939 sealed the fate of millions of European Jews, it also brought mass Canadian mobilization for the war effort. The organized Jewish community responded with recruitment drives to encourage Jewish men to enlist in the Canadian military. It was with great pride that Jewish volunteers marched down the middle of College to the cheers of flag-waving Jewish onlookers. And as their sons went off to war, those left behind worried and worked. And there *was* work to do. The wartime economy banished unemployment and created opportunities for new industry and expansion of existing industry. And everywhere there was war-related activity, even for children. Neighbourhood schools and high schools that served the College Street area – Central Tech, Central Commerce and Harbord Collegiate – organized scrap drives, newspaper collection depots and fundraisers.

Shortly after the war ended in Allied victory in 1945, the Jews of College Street, like the rest of Canada, were caught up in an economic boom. As the Canadian economy expanded, many jobs were going unfilled. As a result, labour-intensive industry demanded that government lift the immigration restrictions imposed in the 1920s and '30s. At the same time, the Jewish community, shaken by the destruction of European Jewry, lobbied the government to allow the remnant of European Jews to enter Canada.

As Canada reopened its doors to immigration, a new wave of Jews, survivors of the Holocaust, arrived on College Street – Jews who were looking for a bright future while nursing wounds of loss and personal torture. The older Jewish community along the street, which had become more Canadianized over the 1920s and '30s, and by the patriotic fervour of war, reacted to these Jews with no small measure of ambivalence. Some of these newly arrived *griner* ("green ones") were family members, *lansleit* from the same towns, or Jews who had suffered as Jews and deserved some support. But many of the *gayle* ("yellow ones," or the Jews who had arrived earlier) were wondering how much support was enough, as their own resources weren't all that substantial and they simply felt *different* from these newcomers, who usually did not speak English and whose experiences were hardly to be believed.

As these new arrivals carved out a place for themselves in the College neighbourhood, they also contributed to the throb of College Street Jewish life. With little money to spend on entertainment, they found it cheap and pleasant to pass a Friday or Saturday evening and perhaps a Sunday afternoon *shpatsiring*, strolling along the north side of College – and it was always the north side – between Spadina and Bathurst. The Jewish parade also afforded survivors the faint hope of chancing on an acquaintance from home or an extended family member who also miraculously survived the Holocaust. And if not that, then College Street was a place to make new friends. It was a place to pick up bits of information and advice on jobs, housing and social activities. And for many it would prove a place for courtship and the renewal of life's family cycle.

Sign for a Jewish butcher in the Ward. Photo:TA

Louis Rasminsky

Louis Rasminsky, a soft-spoken, charming and gifted economist, has often been referred to as one of many unsung heroes in Canada. He was the quiet mastermind behind the International Monetary Fund (IMF) who never took credit for his design that some argue singlehandedly stabilized the global financial system in 1944.

Rasminsky's family moved to Toronto in 1913. The youngest of the family, he attended Lansdowne Public School and Harbord Collegiate, becoming the high school's class valedictorian in 1925. At his matriculation examination, competing against the province's best and brightest, Rasminsky finished first in English, German and History. Continued success at the University of Toronto's Economics Department motivated one of Rasminsky's professors to approach Jewish community leaders with a pitch to establish a scholarship that would send Rasminsky to the London School of Economics. In London, Rasminsky would study under John Maynard Keynes and Harold Laski. Within a year, he had already moved on to the League of Nations in Geneva.

In 1940, Rasminsky joined the Bank of Canada and its Foreign Exchange Control Board. Four years later, he reunited with Keynes at the Bretton Woods conference, the organizational meeting where he eventually created the IMF.

In 1961, Rasminsky beat the odds to become the first Jewish governor of the Bank of Canada. It was sweet vindication after being passed over twice, in 1949 and 1955. In 1968, he received the honour of Companion of the Order of Canada.

The Kiever Synagogue on Bellevue Avenue. Photo: Vincenzo Pietropaolo

Of course, College also remained a place of Jewish business and commerce. Walking down the street, *griner* and *gayle* alike passed the building that housed the office of the Communist Labour Progessive Party's JB Salsberg, whose Yiddish oratory, occasional strong-arm tactics and commitment to human rights won him election to the Provincial Parliament. In the same building, there were no less than eight furriers vying with one another for customers. Several doors down was the Garden Theatre, where the fare was mostly B-grade movies and serials, unlike the classier Bellevue Theatre further west that was home to first-run Hollywood blockbusters. Next door to the Garden Theatre was the Garden Billiard Academy, an upstairs local hangout where a new generation of young men would eat their sunflower seeds and try to look tough. Even further down the street, on the other side of Bathurst between Clinton and Grace, was the Pylon Theatre.

As with billiards, so with other businesses. Through the post-war years, a new generation of professionals and shopkeepers – some the children of those who had laboured in clothing factories – came to College Street. As money became a little easier and eating out more common, a variety of new restaurants also opened along College. Not all these restaurants were successful or even good, but they did afford customers a choice of menu. Some catered to a traditional Jewish palate, while others served more "Canadian" food. In 1950, among the more popular eateries between Spadina and Ossington were the Roumanian Grill, the Paskowitz

Delicatessen, the Mars, the Purity Tea Room, the Victory Restaurant, Tishler's Appetizer Delicatessen, the College Kosher Delicatessen and, on the south side of College at Bathurst, the Daisy Restaurant.

For some of the newly arrived immigrants, who were often short of money, the idea of sitting down to a full meal in a restaurant was an extravagance, even a luxury. For many, the priority was not eating out, but putting food on the table. The *griner*, newly arrived, looked for jobs – any job – to make ends meet. Without connections or fluency in English, it was not always easy. One German Jew with a young family climbed the stairs to the office of JB Salsberg to ask his help in getting a job as a shipping clerk for one of the fancier clothing manufacturers. Salsberg called in a favour from a labour union connection and the German Jewish refugee was hired. A young Polish Jew who had been a slave labourer in a Nazi munitions factory looked to an uncle in Toronto who found him a job soldering silver for a nearby jewellery manufacturer. With more hope than capital, several years later he and his sister tried their hands at running a small gift shop next to the Pylon.

Another young immigrant who had survived the war among the partisans in the forests of Lithuania wrangled a job that he hoped would equip him to become a jeweller. But this fledgling jeweller, like many other *griner*, soon learned that craftsmanship was not enough. He needed to know English. After coming home from work and grabbing a quick dinner, many of these immigrants made their way

CONTINUED PAGE 76

Minding the Store

AN ALBUM OF FAMILY BUSINESSES FROM THE COLLEGE STREET JEWISH COMMUNITY

Caplan Barbershop at 468 College (1935). Photo: JA

Zabrack's Dry Goods at 649 College. Photo: JA

Joseph Gary's Grocery at 420 College (1935). Photo: JA

Vneeda Cigar Store, 824 College (1920). Photo: JA

GROCERIES

DRINK
Coca-Cola

RED ROSE
TEA
"is good tea"

WRIGLEY'S

The Garfinkle store at 302 College.
Photo: AO

north of College to Harbord Collegiate, where they attended intensive evening English classes. Although post-war arrivals struggled to learn English as fast as they could, it was not always fast enough. One former College Street area resident has bittersweet memories of his awkwardness in English. As a treat, he and several friends used to frequent the Daisy Restaurant, where the apple pie and ice cream was especially popular, not just because it was good but because most had only mastered enough English to order "apple pie and ice cream." When he finally and proudly memorized an English phrase permitting him to order a sandwich he liked, he was flummoxed when the waitress responded by asking if he wanted the sandwich "plain or toasted." Not knowing how to respond, he beat a hasty retreat and ordered "apple pie and ice cream."

As the 1950s wore on, these kinds of stories became less and less common. The newcomers learned English and, whether through schools, business, social contact or shared interests, the gulf between the *griner* and *gayle* was gradually bridged. But even as differences between *griner* and *gayle* disappeared on College Street, Jews also began to disappear from the neighbourhood. With increased affluence, more and more Jews began moving away from College and went "up the hill," north of Davenport. "Up the hill" meant success. Even before the Second World War, some better-off Jews had already moved north from the College neighbourhood to the St. Clair West area, where a large synagogue was constructed in the 1940s. But by the 1950s, most Jews were looking still further north. New houses and subdivisions began to spring up north of Eglinton along the Bathurst Street corridor, the new artery of Jewish life. Jewish institutions soon followed. With ongoing Jewish depopulation of the College Street neighbourhood, the Talmud Torah relocated from Brunswick to Bathurst just south of Wilson, and the YM-YWHA first moved to Bloor and Spadina in the mid-1950s, then opened a new, modern and large suburban branch on Bathurst north of Sheppard. By the mid-'60s, most of the big congregations that had dotted the streets that ran off College sold their downtown properties and followed their congregants northward. Some new synagogues, like the large Beth Tzedec on Bathurst south of Eglinton, were formed out of the merger of two or more downtown congregations. Only a few smaller College neighbourhood synagogues remained, struggling to remain open so that observant Jews working downtown could say *kaddish*, the daily prayer recited for the dead.

Some may also have felt it was time to say *kaddish* for Jewish College Street. Most Jewish-owned businesses relocated to areas of new Jewish population concentration, while other Jewish organizations proved less mobile or enduring. Their time had passed and with them much of the Jewish flavour of the area. While Kensington south of College remained a vibrant market area, signs proclaiming Kosher chicken and meat gradually disappeared, as did the crowds of Thursday and Friday Jewish shoppers buying for the Sabbath. And the College streetcar was no longer packed

JB Salsberg

Born in impoverished settings in 1903 in Lagov, Poland, Joseph Baruch (JB) Salsberg came to Canada with his family when he was 11 and settled in the heart of the garment district at Spadina and College. Salsberg attended Lansdowne Public School, but stayed only two years before dropping out to get a job as a leather cutter to help support his family. Although his parents had hoped he would become a rabbi – they themselves helped found the Eitz Chaim Schools – JB instead became drawn to social activism. He regularly attended meetings of the Young Labour Zionists and the United Hat, Cap and Millinery Workers Union.

Salsberg joined the Communist Party in 1926. His foray into city politics began in 1938 when he was elected as a city alderman of Ward 4. He followed this by winning a provincial seat as a Labour Progressive Party candidate, representing the St. Andrews riding.

While sitting in the Ontario Legislature, Salsberg assisted in bringing forth legislation banning discrimination in public places, considered a breakthrough of the time.

By 1957, rumours of suppression of Jewish life in the U.S.S.R. sent Salsberg overseas to meet with Soviet Premier Nikita Kruschev. The Kremlin cautioned Salsberg not to make any public statements, but upon his return, Salsberg wrote exposés of the regime's treacheries. He then resigned from the communist party, an exit that inspired other defections thereby ending the Communist Party's presence as an effective political force in Canada.

Salsberg continued however, to be a leading community figure as contributor to The Canadian Jewish News, chair of the Committee for Yiddish in the early '70s, and eventually helped establish University of Toronto's first Yiddish courses.

College looking west to Grace. 1959. Photo: Scotiabank Group Archives

with Jewish workers coming and going from the clothing factories that had once been the economic mainstay of the College Street community. Without Jewish workers, the once-Jewish – even Yiddish-speaking – character of Toronto's clothing workers' unions also began to pass into history.

The exodus of Jews from their former College Street neighbourhood is almost complete. There are only a few visible Jewish presences on a street once dominated by Jews. High on the side of a building near the southeast corner of College and Spadina, faded paint recalls this was once the place of business of the H. Eisen Bag Co. A Jewish optometrist from the 1950s has stayed in business on College Street, passing the offices from father to son. And the Bagel Restaurant is the lone forlorn reminder of the many Jewish restaurants that

once served the surrounding College Jewish community.

There are, however, flutterings of new Jewish life in the College Street area. An explosion of condominiums, retrofitted factories and renovated apartments have come onto the market, fuelling the lure of growth in Toronto's downtown core. As a result, a new generation of Jews and others are making their way back to College Street. Once-struggling downtown congregations have been given a new lease on life. A College Street restaurant between Bathurst and Spadina is feeding the "New Jewish Culture" with "a traditional Jewish Sunday brunch" accompanied by live klezmer music. And much to the surprise of the young survivor who studied to be a jeweller, his daughter, who recently joined the family's successful diamond import business, has moved into a

fashionable condominium on College only a few minutes' walk from where her immigrant father first found a place to live. Perhaps College Street may not only have a Jewish past. Maybe it has a Jewish future as well. And perhaps then, it may yet be too soon to say *kaddish* for a Jewish presence on College.

Johnny Lombardi (Forza Roma) and friends.
Photo courtesy of Lenny Lombardi.

College Street Little Italy

More than a Century of Toronto Italia[1]

GABRIELE SCARDELLATO

Italian family in the Ward (1913). Photo: TA

One of the best students of the lives of migrants and immigrants in Canada, and the doyen of Italian-Canadian studies in particular – Robert F. Harney – considered the Little Italy that developed on College Street between Bathurst Street and Ossington Avenue, in the city's west side, to be one of the most important immigrant settlements in Toronto. For Harney, in fact, this Little Italy was so important as to present itself as a model for how one might study the general urban immigrant experience in Canada.[2] In his effort to develop that model and to write a history of "Toronto Italia," Harney suggested that the best strategy might be to read the immigrants as "texts." In other words, he proposed that we approach the immigrant experience through the lives of its protagonists by allowing them to speak for themselves as much as possible. This strategy seems promising and serves as a useful guide for this attempt to produce a history of College Street Little Italy.

Migrants and immigrants from Italy have been present in Toronto from very early in the city's history, but a large Italian-origin population did not emerge until the closing years of the 19th century, and the early years of the 20th. By the late 1890s, emigration rates from Italy (for all destinations) reached truly astonishing levels, as Italians fled in ever larger numbers from *miseria*: the social and economic misery in their homeland caused by appalling conditions for which they could see no solutions. At the beginning of the last century, their departure rates came to total more than half a million every year in a population of some 33 million. In that vast movement of people – made up of both temporary migrants (or sojourners) and immigrants – North America became the most important destination, and it became so just as internal economic and political conditions in Italy were changing the regions with the highest emigration rates within the country from north to south.

Canada, of course (and Montreal and Toronto in particular), became an important destination for Italians in this period. In the early 1890s, there were only about 3,000 residents in Canada who were of Italian origin, but this figure grew substantially in the years before the First World War, and by the end of Italian emigration in the early 1970s, it had reached about 750,000. At the current level of about 1.3 million, the population total reached by the end of the era of emigration has almost doubled again. Over the same period, the Italian-origin population of Toronto grew from far less than 1,000 to the current total of almost 500,000. Indeed, as many have observed, Toronto's Italian-origin population has grown to become one of the largest and most significant outside of Italy, and the role of the city's College Street Little Italy proved crucial in that development.

Almost from the beginning of their journeys to Toronto, Italians developed a relatively complex pattern of settlement based on factors like their villages, towns or provinces of origin in Italy; the economic niches they were able to fill in the city; and their proximity both to places of work and to transportation facilities. The result, by the early years of the last century, was a series of at least four main settlement areas. The largest of these, and arguably the most important, was located in the area of the city then known as the Ward, a name derived from St. John's Ward, one of the early city electoral districts bounded by College and Queen streets to the north and south respectively and by Yonge Street to the east and University Avenue in the west. Another concentration of Italian settlement developed somewhat further north and to the west of the Ward in the neighbourhood of Dufferin Street near Davenport Avenue, and over time this settlement expanded westward to reach the West Toronto Junction and south as far as Wallace Street. A third settlement, albeit somewhat smaller than these two, developed to the east of the Ward, in the area around the intersection of Queen Street East and Parliament Street. Finally, the fourth settlement area that developed – also relatively near to the Ward – is the one that is most important for our purposes. The area bounded by College and Dundas streets on the north and south respectively and by Grace Street in the west and Euclid Avenue to the east was the original heart of College Street Little Italy. It was from this centre that it would grow to become the post-Second World War heart of Toronto Italia.

The beginnings of an Italian presence in this neighbourhood can be traced to the 1890s and the settlements there by a number of immigrants from Calabria, in particular from the town of Rende and its surrounding municipalities in the province of Cosenza. One of the earliest of these immigrants was Salvatore Turano, who settled on Mansfield (what was then Cowan) Avenue, where he established a grocery store,

The Way of the Cross procession.
Photo courtesy of St. Francis Church

The Societá Italo Canadese Band of Toronto at the 5th Annual Picnic, Long Branch (June 4, 1923). Photo: AO

boarding house and labour agency. Some of the paesani for whom he provided housing and for whom he found work – many on city road and street railway construction – also began to settle in the neighbourhood, as did other entrepreneurs, like Rafaelle Bartello and (somewhat later) Carmine Spizzirri, also on Mansfield Avenue, and Pasquale Molinaro, who settled on Gore Street. Vincenzo Muto, another Calabrian, was also an early migrant to the area when, in 1910, he moved his tailor shop from his D'Arcy Street address, just west of the Ward, to a new location on College Street near Grace. At about the same time, Francesco Tomaiuolo, "one of the city's most influential padroni, who was primarily a private banker and steamship agent,"

also settled in the neighbourhood, where he constructed a multi-purpose building, "a modern, decorous bank and retail outlet, and small hotel," the Venezia Hotel (later known as the Monarch), located at the corner of Henderson Avenue and Clinton Street.[3] From this facility he conducted his affairs as a private banker and moneychanger, a travel agent, a newsagent (Italian-language newspapers, calendars, postcards and stamps) and a vendor of gramophone records and harmonicas. For about two years, he also published his own newspaper, *Il Progresso Italo-Canadese* (1929-1931), edited by his brother. Tomaiuolo's bank clientele provides a valuable insight into the population of the emerging College Street Little Italy in the first decades of the last century. Not

surprisingly, more than half of them were Calabrians while others were from Basilicata, Sicily, Molise and Apulia, and almost all had settled in the nearby streets around Toma-iuolo's Venezia Hotel.

Through the settlement of first hundreds and then thousands of immigrants, College Street Little Italy grew just as the earlier concentration of Italian settlement in the Ward dispersed and declined. This earlier settlement and its commingling of Jews, Italians and other immigrants had served as a first reception area because of its proximity to transportation systems, affordable (if disreputable) housing and other amenities. It was never well-accepted, however, and when city authorities began to dismantle it to make way

CONTINUED PAGE 86

The Italo Canadese Society of Toronto on Clinton Street,
south of College; the epicentre of Little Italy, 1927

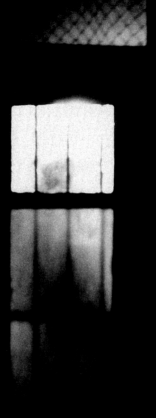

Gino and the Clinton Shoe Repair.
Photo: Francis Crescia

OPPOSITE: The Italo Canadese Society (Detail)
Photo: Panoramic Photo Co.

ABOVE : Poet Mastro Vito Papa reading at the Christmas party of Circolo Le Caravelle (1975).

LEFT: The Circolo Le Caravelle. Mr. Vincenzo Pascale, president, fourth from left, front row. Photos: Vincenzo Pietropaolo

for redevelopment – for example, the construction of the Toronto General Hospital beginning in 1910 – its inhabitants moved on, and one of the destinations for Italians, as suggested by Vincenzo Muto's tailor shop, was the College Street neighbourhood. Of course, the dispersal took place over a considerable length of time, and even after it had been completed, traces of the earlier presence, in or near the Ward, remained. The most conspicuous of these was the church of the first Italian national parish, Our Lady of Mt. Carmel, on St. Patrick Street north of Dundas. Less obvious is a bronze plaque depicting a laurel crown dedicated to Italian Canadians and placed in 1922 by the Societá Italo-Canadese on the Edith Cavell Monument located on University Avenue

south of College.[4]

While some of these landmarks survived and continued to attract those who had created them, others were also established for similar purposes. These, however, were created in the area that increasingly was coming to be known as home – in the vicinity of College and Clinton streets – for more and more Italians in Toronto. In 1913, for example, as Tomaiuolo and others were establishing themselves in the neighbourhood, Italian immigrants were granted the church of St. Agnes, at the intersection of Grace and Dundas, as the second Italian national parish in the city. Their predecessors, Irish and other English-speaking Roman Catholics, moved further north on Grace Street to the newly constructed (1908)

church of St. Francis.[5] In the following decade, the last during which any significant emigration occurred before the Depression and the Second World War,[6] the Italian-origin population of this newer Little Italy grew to about 2,500, with a central group of about 400 Calabrians settled, as we have seen, around Mansfield Avenue. As suggested in Tomaiuolo's client list, there were also smaller groupings from other Italian regions who established themselves in the area: the Apulians also settled on Mansfield Avenue and nearby, at its intersection with Manning Avenue and somewhat further away, on Markham Street, between College and Dundas; immigrants from Latium (Sora in particular) on Claremont Street; and settlers from Pisticci, Basilicata,

Photo: Vincenzo Pietropaolo

on Henderson Avenue and also on Euclid south of College, to name only the most numerous.[7] A survey of College Street between Grace and Bathurst conducted in 1926 reported that more than 60 per cent of the businesses on the street were Italian or used Italian in their names. To appreciate the vigorous growth that the neighbourhood experienced during these years, we must add to this considerable presence those establishments that were located in the immediate vicinity of College Street itself, as well as the significant concentration of settlement that was also developing, despite the fact that immigration effectively had ended. By the 1930s, the Italian-origin population of this settlement has been estimated at about 10,000 (in a city-wide total of about 13,000, according to the 1931 federal census).[8] By the beginning of the Second World War, then, this neighbourhood had become the heart of Toronto Italia, and we can gain some precious insights, generally suggestive of everyday realities for its residents, through memories preserved for us by some of the descendants of the first settlers.

Dominic Vaccaro, for example, was an immigrant from the Basilicata region of Italy who worked for some time in Peterborough, Ontario, before moving to and settling in Toronto, on Bellwoods Avenue, south of Dundas, before the First World War. An injury had left him lame and the only way he could earn a living, according to his granddaughter, Mary Caruso, was by playing the barrel organ or hurdy-gurdy at various street corners in the city. Like many other immigrants of the time, Vaccaro anglicized his name, and became, perhaps in a self-conscious reference to his injury, Dominic Walker. By the early 1920s, when he was well-established, he had developed a successful daily routine. He attended mass every morning at St. Agnes Church and then at 11:00 a.m. he set off with his barrel organ, "always walking everywhere," to return eventually at midnight. Except for days "when the weather was bad and he couldn't get out," he followed his routine six days out of seven. "He'd stay the whole day at the one corner and change to another the next day. Saturday was Queen and Bathurst because of all of the shoppers in the area." This routine ensured "a good living" for himself and

Reverend Riccardo Polticchia.
Photo: Vincenzo Pietropaolo

OPPOSITE: St. Agnes Church.
Photo courtesy St. Francis Church

his family, recalls Caruso. "Some days he'd make a good few dollars – $12 or $13. A poor day was only $4 or $5. ..." Caruso remembers that Vaccaro was well-known in his own community on Bellwoods Avenue and on the nearby streets in part because of an extended family of both maternal and paternal aunts and uncles and other relatives.[9]

Any number of immigrant lives might be selected to illustrate the development of College Street Little Italy in the decade before the mass migration of Italians that occurred after the Second World War. Two such lives in particular, however, provide us with glimpses as important as those contained in Mary Caruso's oral history of her grandfather. Another immigrant family from Pisticci, Basilicata, settled in the neighbourhood before the Second World War. Leonardo and Teresa Barbalinardo arrived in Toronto before the First World War and spent some time living in difficult conditions in the Ward, moving from rooming house to rooming house. Their first child, a son who would grow to become one of the best-known residents of College Street Little Italy, was born in one of these rooming houses, "on a kitchen table," in December 1915. The family lived in extreme poverty and eventually, like many others, moved out of the Ward to join the growing settlement near College and Clinton streets.

The son, Giovanni Barbalinardo – or Johnny Lombardi, as he became known – grew up in the neighbourhood where he lived and prospered his entire life. He made a career for himself as a young trumpet player and bandleader, served in the Canadian Armed Forces in the Second World War,

became a grocer at the corner of Manning and Dundas on his return after the war, married and started a family in the 1950s, premiered an Italian-language radio program, began his own radio station in 1966 – and the rest, as they say, is history, including a laudable career as a philanthropist. Johnny Lombardi's accomplishments and contributions to the lives of his community and to contemporary multicultural Toronto have been recognized by the city in the renaming of a section of College Street as Johnny Lombardi Way.[10] Part of Lombardi's importance for this study lies in the role that he, and others like him, played as a bridging generation for the new immigrants who began to arrive in greater and greater numbers beginning in the 1950s.

Another who played a similar role, though now perhaps less well-known publicly, was Julius Molinaro, the son of Pasquale Molinaro, whose settlement with other Calabrians in College Street Little Italy in the second decade of the last century has already been described. Pasquale Molinaro worked as a motorman for the Toronto Transit Commission and was also the local reporter for the New York-based *Progresso Italo-Americano*. Julius Molinaro, together with his brother Frank, grew up as a strong admirer of Italy and all things Italian, a passion that he nurtured through an undergraduate and then two graduate degrees at the nearby University of Toronto.

Molinaro completed a very successful career as a professor of Italian Studies at his alma mater, but for an Italian Canadian it was a career that included considerable chal-

lenges. Like many others of his era, Molinaro was subjected to harsh treatment in June 1940, when Italian dictator Benito Mussolini declared war on Great Britain and its allies, including Canada. Many Italian Canadians, often regardless of their citizenship or place of birth, were arrested, and eventually over 500 were interned as suspected Fascist sympathizers and possible so-called "fifth columnists." Among these were Julius Molinaro and his father and brother. Ironically, perhaps, Molinaro served in the Canadian Armed Forces after four and one-half months of internment, and after he was discharged he resumed his career at the University of Toronto.[11] Clearly, experiences like these had an important effect on Italians not only in Toronto's Little Italy but also in Canada in general, no doubt influencing – probably with caution and some hesitation – their ability to greet post-war newcomers and to help them negotiate their encounter with the Canadian mainstream.

In the aftermath of the Second World War, Italy experienced another mass emigration from the late 1940s to the mid-'70s. Some 7 million of its inhabitants departed after the war; half a million of these made their way to Canada and about 70 per cent of this total were from southern Italy. In Italy itself there was a further population shift (generally from south to north) of some 9 million internal migrants. In descending order, those who emigrated abroad came from the following Italian regions: Calabria, Sicily, Abruzzi, Molise, Latium, Veneto and Campania. The war had served to further devastate an economy already in trouble in the 1920s

**Visiting Italian traffic officer demonstrates his technique.
Photo: Vincenzo Pietropaolo (1975)**

and '30s and, as in earlier periods, few Italians could see any hope for the future. At the same time, countries like Canada emerged with a strong need to rebuild sectors of their economies that had been neglected in wartime. This need coincided with those of Canadian citizens, in particular returning service people and their families who had also been held in check because of wartime priorities. As the Canadian economy expanded after the war, it experienced a need for labour, and that need coincided with those in devastated countries like Italy who were weighing their futures.

Beginning first under so-called "bulk," or contract labour, programs sponsored by the government, including a short-lived effort to import young Italian women as domestics, and then increasingly through the mechanism of chain migra-

tion and family sponsorship and reunification, annual Italian emigration to Canada grew to unprecedented levels.[12] The first arrivals in Canada generally were lone males (both married and single) who had contracted for one year of labour before they could be free to either stay or return. Most chose to stay. In Toronto, the primary receiving neighbourhood for this new influx was College Street Little Italy, which, over a relatively short period, extended its boundaries considerably, from Bloor Street in the north to beyond Queen Street in the south and from Bathurst Street in the east to beyond Dovercourt in the west. The arriving Italian immigrants who were responsible for this expansion arguably were the most "visible" of the immediate post-Second World War immigrant influx to Toronto; they played an important role

in the transformation of the city from "Toronto the Good" to "Toronto the World in a City." From early on, both difficulties and challenges were encountered in the accommodation of an ever-growing immigrant population, and these often were resolved by the immigrants themselves.

One of the most significant challenges was housing. Fortunato Rao arrived in 1952 and settled for a time on Brunswick Avenue, in the top floor of a house shared with a Jewish family. Rao "shopped on Queen Street because College Street was more expensive. ... We shopped at Lombardi's and south on Claremont Street," he later recalled. "We were so happy to find Italian products." Later, Rao moved to a residence he shared with a cousin on Clinton Street and nearby, on Manning Avenue, about "28 men, five per room,"

Photo: Vincenzo Pietropaolo (1975)

lived in one house. The men cooked for themselves on a "stove in the basement with four burners."[13] Of course, these early arrivals would have preferred more substantial and less crowded accommodation, but often their means were limited just as their ambitions were focused on other goals. Within days, if not hours, of their arrival, they were at work, intent on putting to use what was often the only resource available to them and the only resource that made their emigration possible: their labour. Many of them were intent on paying off debts encountered during their immigration; others struggled to save enough to pay for their families to join them or to be able to marry (often by proxy) and to begin their own families; still others were already saving for the all-important purchase of a first home. So labourers arriving

alone might find accommodation with relatives already housed (albeit themselves saving to move on to better conditions) or share quarters with others from the village or town.

Contemporary observers from outside the group (and occasionally even those on the inside) were sometimes shocked by the conditions they thought prevailed in Little Italy. Fortunately, others went beyond surface appearances in their efforts to understand the lives of those they were describing. In 1961, for example, after a decade of substantial Italian immigration to Little Italy, the late Pierre Berton, accomplished journalist and historian, published a series of articles in the Toronto *Daily Star*, describing, on the basis of first-hand experience by a colleague, the then Liberal Member of the Provincial Parliament for Dovercourt Riding,

Andrew Thompson, the experiences of three newly arrived families. All three families – the Moscones, the Roccos and the Gasparis – a total of 12 people, shared a narrow (14-foot wide) house with three small apartments and two kitchens between them. Their diet was extremely limited, although the journalist observed, "nobody went hungry." One of the families owned a radio and used it sporadically to listen exclusively to Italian-language broadcasting, but they had not been to a cinema after their arrival in Canada. All but one of the immigrants, however – men, women and children – who shared this house and this humble lifestyle, worked.

The men leave in the morning, often before 6:30 a.m., and do not return until supper. The wives also vanish during the day. Clelia

For many people, Little Italy will always be linked with the Lombardi family. Lenny Lombardi works as President and CEO of CHIN Radio/TV International, where he has developed and expanded on ethnic radio and television broadcasting in Canada under the expert guidance and inspiration of his late father Johnny Lombardi. Like his father before him, Lenny plays a central role in the life of Little Italy. He is the Chairperson of the Little Italy Business Association, the executive producer of the world famous CHIN Picnic, and he is one of the chief organizers of the Taste of Little Italy Festival in June and the Fiera Festival in September. Keeping with family tradition, Lenny sits on many boards and has helped raise funds for many charities. Through his work in broadcasting Lenny has taken his experience in College Street community building and applied it to the many ethnocultural communities served on CHIN RADIO.

Nicola Riga with son Bruno in the backyard of 206 Grace St., 1965.

Moscone, for instance, leaves at 7 a.m. to work scrubbing floors … for $7 a day. Mrs. Virgilio Rocco leaves for work at Mario's restaurant at 10:30 a.m. and doesn't return home until six. She leaves again at 11 and works until 3 a.m. She is paid $25 a week. Mrs. Ferno [sic] Gaspari … works in a laundry. Young Natalino Moscone, aged 14, works for 50 cents an hour as a drugstore delivery boy. … His brother, Attilio, is expected to work during the summer holidays as a shoeshine boy.[14]

When the research for the three-part series was carried out, Dominic Moscone had been unemployed for more than 18 months. "For an Italian," Berton concluded, "being unemployed is tragic."

Like the families described here, Rao and other immigrants were intent on "making do" and working hard

to achieve their immigrant dreams. Rao continued to live in Little Italy while he worked first on the west side, on Roselawn Avenue, and then in Scarborough (at Kennedy Road north of Eglinton), a two-hour commute from home, and then at Dupont Street and Ossington Avenue, on the border of the Junction settlement, where he was employed by the American Standard Company. For Rao, as for many others, the neighbourhood was a temporary but extremely important sojourn. Within four years of his arrival in Little Italy, he had moved on to North York, where he settled and, in 1959, was able to buy his own home.

Also like many others, however, Rao's memories of College Street as the locus for insertion into mainstream society are bittersweet. One of the common experiences, for example, together with housing, employment and other challenges,

Ciccolini Brothers

When the Ciccolini brothers and their mother arrived in Canada in 1956, they were coming to join their father for a new start to a new life in Toronto. Their early experience of living here was "perhaps the biggest character-building time" for them and their entire family, as Max and Sam Ciccolini recall. "For us, 'Little Italy' was the catalyst for the future of our family," Max says.

Growing up in Little Italy, the brothers worked before and after school. "Regardless of our age," Max says, "as members of a new immigrant family, it was understood that we had to help out my father in a household of five children." They took on two large paper routes, delivering the *Globe & Mail* early in the morning before school, and then worked as delivery boys for a nearby pharmacy in the evenings after school.

Life in Little Italy wasn't all work all the time, of course. Max says he won't forget how as a kid, while working at Cappe's Drug Store at 710 College, he and his brother were often asked by Sam Sniderman (a.k.a. Sam the Record Man) to bring the current 78 RPM records to Johnny Lombardi's radio station at Grace and College for him to play on his show.

"The character-building and experience of those years," Max says, "were the very foundation of our successful business and family lives."

And what successes they have had. Besides building up a flourishing company together called Masters Insurance, which Sam and brother Frank started in 1968, the Ciccolini family has had a good 30 years of involvement and activity within the Italian and wider community, including playing a vital role within the local organization Villa Charities.

For his entrepreneurial and philanthropic accomplishments, Sam received the Order of Ontario in 1999, and then the prestigious Order of Canada in 2005. When interviewed about this distinction, Sam attributed his successes in life to their childhood growing up while working in the Little Italy community. "It really gave us a good upbringing, a solid foundation."

Vincenzo, Mario and Carlo. Photo: Francis Crescia

Bruna Crescia, Assunta Patrina, Maria Plati.
Photo: Francis Crescia

Nivo Angelone

"I've given my life to this community." That's how Nivo Angelone describes his involvement in Little Italy. The list of activities this current president of the Italian Chamber of Commerce of Toronto has played a vital role in since moving here in 1971 certainly gives good reason for his sentiment.

Ask anyone who was as involved as Angelone was in the 1970s and they will tell you just how much Angelone devoted himself to this community. Ask Angelone himself, and he hardly knows where to begin.

Angelone helped run the Centro Organizzativo Italiano at College and Beatrice, giving free assistance to new immigrants and organizing thousands of unemployed and injured workers. Many of the nonviolent demonstrations he organized to fight for workers' rights were huge successes, like the mass at St. Francis Church for May Day 1973. He was also involved with the Associazione Democratica Italiana and the International Ladies' Garment Union.

Angelone had a hand, too, in running a theatre group called the Compagnia dei Giovani, which brought plays to the community when it was lacking in cultural activities.

What stood out about Angelone was that he always made it a point to encourage those he was organizing to take control of their own lives.

"I've never been the leader," he says. "I always let someone else emerge to take the lead."

Angelone saw the discontentment in the community at the time, and he saw his purpose in empowering the disempowered, engaging the disengaged and helping people realize they had the power to change their own lives for the better.

In all his years of activism and community involvement, Angelone never considered running for office, even though many people along the way have tried to convince him to do so. He says he refuses to get involved in the power struggle inherent in politics. Instead, he has always wanted to stay close to the community. And that's exactly what he has done for the past 35 years and will continue to do for the years to come.

was the encounter with public space in "Toronto the Good" in the post-Second World War period. According to Rao, "[W]e were three or four of us on the sidewalk and saw the police, we would take off because if we stayed they would say, 'Disperse.' … The police used to say, 'Split it up.' I recall we used to go to the Monarch bar and the other one at Spadina Avenue and College Street…."[15]

This treatment by local authorities seems inconceivable on the streets of Toronto today and above all on the streets of Little Italy where, weather permitting, café life spills onto the sidewalks. That it does so is part of the cultural legacy of those immigrants who eventually protested the treatment they received and were able to introduce new possibilities for Canadian city life.[16] Despite hostilities of this type, the newcomers found considerable institutional support to meet their needs and they also quickly began to add to those institutions either by beginning their own enterprises or making use of those already in place. New grocery stores and similar enterprises (travel agencies, news agencies, butcher shops, bakeries and so forth) were added, helping to meet the needs of an expanding population.

The *Corriere Canadese* appeared on the scene in the early 1950s. Its first newsroom was located at College and Major streets, while its editorial office was located to the west at Heydon Park Road and its administrative offices nearby on Brock Avenue near to its intersection with the western end of College Street. The first version of the paper appeared as a result of the efforts of Arturo Scotti, Gianni Grohovaz,

Sam Sorbara, Joseph Carrier and others, some of whom were descendants of the earlier, pre-Second World War immigration. The first issue appeared in late 1953, but it did not begin to publish on a regular basis until April of the following year, by which time it had been taken over by the late Dan Ianuzzi and Arturo Scotti. It has survived and flourished to the present alongside a wide range of more short-lived newspapers, including the weekly *Panorama*, *Il Giornale di Toronto*, *Il Tevere* and *Forze Nuove*.[17] In the pages of these publications, we can gain useful insights about daily life in a burgeoning Little Italy.

Theatres in the neighbourhood, for example, were multi-purpose venues where Italian films were screened and a variety of theatrical productions were mounted. The Pylon Theatre (now the Royal) on College Street was one such important venue, together with others like the nearby Studio Cinema (at College and Manning), while somewhat further afield entertainment could also be found at the Paradise Cinema on Bloor near Dovercourt or at the Radio City Cinema on St. Clair at Bathurst, to name some of the better known movie houses. In December 1958, these four cinemas were screening respectively *Passione Fatale*, *Il Bravo di Venezia*, *I Sogni nel Cassetto* and *I Promessi Sposi*.[18] One new arrival to the neighbourhood (he settled on Markham Street with his sister and brother-in-law in the mid-1950s) saw his first film in Canada "at the Pylon Theatre…. It was called *Il Piccolo Alpino* and I had seen it many years before in Chions (Friuli)." Further, the same newcomer remembered that

**Community meeting to discuss the
Unemployment Insurance Commission. West
End YMCA, 1973.
Photo: Vincenzo Pietropaolo**

Pietropaolo Family

Vince Pietropaolo's entire family has been active in the College Street Italian community for so long now, he can hardly get a grasp on the number of years they have spent working and organizing and volunteering here. Since they immigrated here in 1959 from Calabria, they have put in 30 odd years of continuous activity in this neighbourhood, inspired by their father Paolo, who was a founding member of Circolo Le Caravelle.

For Vince and his brothers Damiano and Domenico, the 1970s was busy with organizing. Vince himself managed three major initiatives: an Italian film festival, held at the Centro Circolo Caravelle on College, that was then billed as the first event of its kind; a summer Italian cultural school program for elementary-school-aged kids, held at St. Lucy's School on Clinton; and what he says was the very first film "about Italians, by Italians," called *Franco, the Story of an Immigrant*, which he helped direct right on College Street.

"I think we caused quite a stir on College Street," Vince says.

Damiano and Domenico caused quite a stir with their activities too. The two were active players at the Centro Organizzativo Italiano on College at Beatrice. With the COI, which was at the centre of political organizing and activism for the Italian and working community in the '70s, the two helped newcomers in their transition into life and work here. They also organized mass meetings that pulled in people by the hundreds, including government officials, to talk about labour issues affecting community members at the time.

These days, the Pietropaolos have found their own professional niches. Vince went from planning to photographing the city, telling the stories of immigrants and workers who remain voiceless in the city; Damiano joined CBC Radio and has become a major producer; Domenico is a professor and chair of the Italian Studies department at the University of Toronto; and Mary, an ESL teacher, has taught new immigrants for many years in the area.

many "singers from Italy, like Claudio Villa, Luciano Taioli and Nilla Pizzi, to mention just a few, helped to alleviate our homesickness. When the enterprising Johnny Lombardi organized such a show, a sell-out was guaranteed."[19] The local theatres served both as cinemas and as venues for dramatic performances or, as noted above, for spectacles sponsored by local impresarios.[20]

Theatrical performances were available almost from the beginning of the post-Second World War immigration to College Street. Bruno Mesaglio and others were active from the early 1950s. The Gruppo Filodrammatico of St. Agnes, who used the parish hall as their base, was the first such group, and on May 6, 1951, the players presented Eduardo De Filippo's *Non Ti Pago*, directed by Ontario Sarracini with "the principal actor … newcomer Bruno Mesaglio." From this initiative was born the famous Piccolo Téatro Italiano, which entertained newcomers and those better established, as well as a wider audience drawn from the host society. From the early 1950s to the '70s they performed in various venues – a production of Morais' *L'Avvocato Difensore*, for example, at the Pylon, in 1954, and Goldoni's *La Locandiera* at the same venue in December 1958 – and also in the parish halls of churches like St. Agnes and St. Mary of the Angels, and at Hart House at the University of Toronto and at Brandon Hall (near St. Mary of the Angels).[21]

The parish church of St. Agnes, served during these years by the Franciscans, was clearly a central institution in the life of the growing Italian neighbourhood after the Second World War, just as it had been in the interwar period. Giuseppe Simonetta remembers the church as an essential resource for newly arrived immigrants like himself (1958), for whom it served as an important point of reference while newcomers found their bearings and began to negotiate their entry into the new host society. The mass immigration after the Second World War, however, quickly put a great strain on the ability of St. Agnes to serve the needs of its parishioners.[22] A solution was found, beginning in 1958, with the provision of Italian-language services at the church of St. Francis of Assisi, at the corner of Mansfield Avenue and Grace Street, near St. Agnes.

Eventually, the Italian national parish itself was moved to St. Francis in 1968, by which time several other churches

in the greatly expanded neighbourhood – St. Helen, on Dundas near its intersection with Lansdowne Avenue, for example, and St. Anthony on Bloor between Dufferin Street and Dovercourt Road – also had begun to offer services in Italian.[23] A few years after the Italian language began to be heard in St. Francis, some of its parishioners resumed a type of religious celebration – in the form of processions with the statues of saints and other figures from the Roman Catholic liturgy – that had formed an important part of their spirituality before immigrating. These began with processions to celebrate the feast of the Madonna of Canneto, of St. Francis of Assisi and so forth, and from these early undertakings emerged one of the most important and signature events of contemporary Little Italy, the annual Good Friday procession during the Easter observances.

The first of these processions, staged in 1962, was a rather humble affair organized by a dedicated committee comprised mostly of immigrants from Calabria.[24] These early processions were held without permission from city authorities, but as their size and popularity spread – with more and more participants in the procession and more and more spectators in attendance – it fell to organizers like Simonetta to "legalize" the event with the authorities. The procession has grown to be the largest of its kind in North America, with the participation of more than 60 organizations, including some who come from other areas of Canada, from the United States and from Italy itself. For dedicated volunteers like Simonetta, the procession has come to symbolize the post-Second World War settlement experience in the new world and, in particular, settlement in Little Italy. Today, the procession brings back to the neighbourhood thousands of immigrants (and their descendants) who have long since left for other corners of the city and beyond.[25]

Ironically perhaps, as the popularity of events like the Good Friday procession was increasing through the early 1960s, the heyday of College Street as an immigrant reception and settlement neighbourhood was already past its prime. The Italian-origin population, using the boundaries of College and Dundas streets on the north and south and Bathurst and Dovercourt in the east and west respectively, had grown to roughly 16,500 in a city-wide population of some 140,000.[26] This reality was evident to observers both in-

side and outside of Little Italy. Writing in 1964, for example, a journalist for *Maclean's* magazine noted, "Little Italy, if the term is applied to the small, congested areas of stores, movies and streets of closely packed semi-detached houses which has its centre around College and Bathurst Streets, and which until 1950 contained most of the Italians in Toronto, is still there. But now it is a funnel through which immigrants pass to an enormous area of Italian concentration one and a half miles wide and four deep that thrusts north through central Toronto beyond the city limits."[27]

The same observer was amazed to discover that his "Torontonian prejudices" that had prepared him to see an Italian immigrant either as a labourer in soiled clothing or "as a swarthy, sinister fellow with hooded eyes" were unfounded. Despite this realization, however, and a general sense of accommodation of the immigrant "other," this was still a host-society generation that was shocked by its increasingly widespread encounter with the Italian immigrants in its midst: "Coffee shops are usually noisy with six or seven men of all ages talking endlessly and as if they are all fighting."[28]

In the early '60s, then, Italian-style bars or *caffé* were still described as "coffee shops" in mainstream Canadian society, but this recognition changed over time, in part due to deliberate marketing strategies by entrepreneurs in Little Italy. The Caffé Diplomatico (then known as the Bar Diplomatico) is one of the best-known landmarks of contemporary College Street Little Italy, a creation of its proprietors, the

Sophia Loren receives royal treatment from a huge crowd of fans on College Street. Photo: OA

Mastrangelo family, including impresario and entrepreneur Rocco Mastrangelo and his brother Paul. After almost 50 years in the neighbourhood, Rocco has described with pride his role in introducing the outdoor, sidewalk patio with its signature sun umbrellas when he took over the bar in the late 1960s.[29]

Mastrangelo began his career in the neighbourhood in the late '50s, when he emigrated from his native province of Foggia, in the region of Apulia, to join his family already settled, in 1952, on Toronto's Grace Street. At first Mastrangelo was dismayed by life in College Street Little Italy. His family, like many others, endured crowded housing conditions, a difficult climate and a less than welcoming host society, and immediately after his arrival he was determined to return to Italy. Instead, his father challenged him to stay and make something of himself. Mastrangelo accepted the challenge and, in the process, and much to his delight, he grew to appreciate the vitality of the neighbourhood in which he chose to pursue his career, in particular "the almost folkloric festival of we Italians from all the regions of Italy" who met on College Street. In the course of his career in the neighbourhood, Mastrangelo has been the proprietor of the Pylon Theatre, Bar (Café) Diplomatico, Lansdowne Theatre and the MVP video and music store. He has also been responsible for bringing many famous Italian performers to Toronto.

In the 1960s, however, as his business interests in the

neighbourhood were expanding and beginning to bear fruit, he was well aware of the shift occurring away from College Street. The Bar Diplomatico, which he established in 1968, was not the first that had appeared in the neighbourhood, but the introduction of the sidewalk patio was a wonderful innovation soon copied by many others. According to Mastrangelo, however, the patio licence alone was not enough – it was also crucial to have an accompanying liquor licence and to encourage, often by paying them modest sums, attractive young women to frequent the patio![30] Despite successes like these, changes in the neighbourhood continued and indeed accelerated over the course of the '70s.

Giovanna Luongo Manni, who had immigrated as a young child in the 1950s and who grew up in the neighbourhood, remembers in vivid detail her childhood experiences and also the changes she has witnessed. Luongo Manni is the very successful restaurateur of Giovanna Trattoria on College, a few doors distant from its intersection with Grace Street.[31] Her father arrived in 1952 from the province of Avellino, in the region of Campania, and he was followed a year later by his wife and two daughters, including Giovanna. At first they lived in a small house on Nassau Street in Kensington Market. Like many of their contemporaries, after a few years of hard work they were able to buy a house on Clinton Street. Eventually they opened their own restaurant on College Street, the Vesuvio, where pizza – perhaps the most famous of all Neapolitan-Italian foods – was introduced to Toronto

and which remains one of the specialties of the present-day Giovanna Trattoria.

Luongo Manni remembers in great detail her experiences in school in the neighbourhood, beginning with elementary school on Borden Street north of the Market, and then moving to Clinton Street, where most of her classmates were Jews, reflecting the large number of Jewish Canadians who still resided in the neighbourhood and would continue to do so until well into the 1960s. Luongo Manni describes Little Italy as "fascinating," a neighbourhood that "started out in the '50s as a landing area where all the Italians came in, and then slowly they started moving out. A few of the smart ones stayed behind, which was good because real estate went high and they integrated well. They didn't go into areas where they became part of a group, part of a ghetto." Her clientele now is mostly non-Italian in origin, and while she feels completely integrated into mainstream Canadian society, she is still upset at being treated as a stereotype rather than being appreciated for the unique – and proud – mixture of cultures she has become.

The neighbourhood changes observed both by those who have remained as residents and by those who continue to work in the area, after having themselves moved away, were well underway even before Luongo Manni's success with Giovanna Trattoria. In the 1970s, for example, almost 36 per cent of a local population of some 34,000 residents, according to the Canadian census, was of Italian-ethnic origin, but

by the end of the last millennium, that figure had dropped to some 17 per cent.[32] Over the same period, the total of those resident in the area that were born in Italy dropped from 24 to 7 per cent – more than a threefold decrease. Perhaps it is not surprising that as this change in the makeup of the neighbourhood occurred, so too did the density of settlement within it. In fact, the "population density dropped by almost 40% [after] 1971, owing largely to the substantial renovations to what were once boarding houses and apartments."[33] In other words, new arrivals in the neighbourhood are no longer those immigrants who were once resigned to endure difficult housing conditions. Having endured, many of those individuals have moved on (more than 90 per cent of Italian immigrants in the City of Toronto, for example, now own their own homes), and those who arrive after them are usually intent on "restoring" the housing stock so that they can enjoy the space from which their predecessors profited.

In the 1980s, as these changes were accelerating, a local business improvement association (BIA) was formed. The association's area of interest spanned the city blocks on College Street between Euclid in the east and Shaw in the west. Within this core segment of College, some 48 per cent "of the roughly 154 businesses ... openly identified with Italy or used the Italian language in their names in 1970. By 2000, the percentage had dropped to 29.2 while businesses with no clear ethnic identification became 64.9 per cent of the total."[34] The BIA sought to counter some of this decline

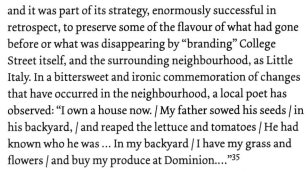

Opposite page left, and this page left,
photo: Vincenzo Pietropaolo
Opposite page right, and this page right
photo: Denis De Klerck

and it was part of its strategy, enormously successful in retrospect, to preserve some of the flavour of what had gone before or what was disappearing by "branding" College Street itself, and the surrounding neighbourhood, as Little Italy. In a bittersweet and ironic commemoration of changes that have occurred in the neighbourhood, a local poet has observed: "I own a house now. / My father sowed his seeds / in his backyard, / and reaped the lettuce and tomatoes / He had known who he was ... In my backyard / I have my grass and flowers / and buy my produce at Dominion...."[35]

A different type of poetry – this time in the Italian language – is presented in a romantic comedy in which Little Italy itself might be said to be a protagonist. This poetry is used as a device in the feature film *Boy Meets Girl*, directed by Jerry Ciccoritti, himself a descendant of the post-Second World War immigration to the neighbourhood. Ciccoritti presents Italian-language poetry in the film as the language of love that, together with other varieties of the Italian language (speech as well as gesture, for example), makes possible a romance between an all-Canadian "boy" and an Italian immigrant "girl." On College Street itself, and at least for the second generation in Little Italy, Ciccoritti's film suggests that over an indeterminate time frame that appears to stretch from the 1960s through the 1990s, Canada meets and falls in love with Italy in a romance that overcomes language and the barriers to understanding and integration that it can symbolize. In other words, for the second and subsequent

generations of Italian Canadians, Little Italy, with its bars, restaurants and other venues, has become a site for romantic encounters. All suggestion of threat posed by the immigrant "other" has dissipated just as the immigrant language itself no longer signifies argument: rather, it has become an essential ingredient for love and romance.

Footnotes

1. Part of the research on which this study is based was made possible through my tenure as the Research Fellow of the Mariano A. Elia Chair in Italian Canadian Studies, York University, and I would like to thank the directors of that institution, in particular Prof. Elio Costa, for their support. I would also like to thank my good friend and colleague Dr. Angelo Principe for his collaboration, in particular with some of the interviews cited below.
2. Robert F. Harney, "Ethnicity and Neighbourhoods," in Robert F. Harney, ed., *Gathering Place: Peoples and Neighbourhoods of Toronto, 1934-1945*, Toronto: Multicultural History Society of Ontario, 1985, for his discussion of how one might study the urban immigrant experience. The importance of Toronto's College Street Little Italy for Harney is also suggested by his family's decision in 1989 to hold his funeral service at the Church of St. Francis of Assisi, in the heart of the neighbourhood.
3. John Zucchi, *Italians in Toronto: Development of a National Identity, 1875-1935*, Kingston and Montreal: McGill-Queen's University Press, 1988, pp. 110-117, for a good description of Tomaiuolo's career, which ended in bankruptcy in 1931.
4 For the laurel wreath, see Angelo Principe, "Italian-Canadian Monuments: A Historical Sketch," in Manuela Scarci and Gabriele Scardellato, eds., *A Monument for Italian-Canadian Immigrants*, Toronto: Dept. of Italian Studies, University of Toronto, and the Italian-Canadian Immigrant Commemorative Association, 1999, p. 3.
5 Zucchi, op cit., chap. 5, for the creation of Toronto's second Roman Catholic Italian national parish; see also R. Perin and G. Scardellato, *Places of Worship in West Toronto*, http://www.yorku.glendon. Father Ezio Marchetto, "The Catholic Church and Italian Immigration to Toronto: An Overview," in *Polyphony: The Bulletin of the Multicultural History Society of Ontario*, vol. 7 no. 1, 1985, pp. 107-110, gives the date for the establishment of St. Francis of Assisi as 1908, and for the creation of St. Agnes as an Italian national parish as 1914.
6 Canadian government restrictions on immigration severely reduced the number of new immigrants to Canada from the early 1920s, and a further

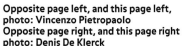

Grace Bagnato

In 1926, the death of a Toronto attorney, Charles Vance Millar, began one of the strangest periods in Canadian history. Millar, who had accumulated a fortune, bequeathed $500,000 of his estate to the Toronto woman who bore the most children within the 10-year period following his death. One of the "contestants" of this "Stork Derby" was Grace Bagnato, who would eventually raise 13 children. Though she didn't win, Bagnato managed to capture the imagination of the Italian community here in Toronto where she lived.

An American by birth, Bagnato and her family moved to Toronto in 1896, settling in the Ward, the isolated ghetto for new immigrants in the city at the time. Bagnato, who spoke English only at first, married a man who spoke Italian only. However, she quickly found that she had a gift for languages, and taught herself Italian along with another six languages that she would become fluent in.

Bagnato began assisting local Italians, Ukrainians, Germans, Poles and anyone else who felt estranged by the new environment. She was an amateur politician and advocate, and even became a court interpreter, unofficially at first until her official appointment in the 1920s.

The Italian community awarded her with an automobile, which was unusual for the time for a woman, in gratitude for her selflessness. Her son Vince described his mother as one of the early seeds of multiculturalism in Canada, reaching as she did out and across so many other communities.

reduction occurred as a result of restrictions on departures from Italy imposed under the dictatorship of Benito Mussolini in Italy from 1928.

7 Franc Sturino, *Forging the Chain: A Case Study of Italian Migration to North America, 1880-1930,* Toronto: Multicultural History Society of Ontario, 1990, chap. 7, "Settler Patterns in Toronto," for estimates about the population and the presence of Calabrians and others. See also Zucchi, op. cit., p. 42.

8 Nick Simone, "Italian Immigrants in Toronto, 1890-1930," Toronto: Dept. of Geography, York University, p. 29, for a report of the 1926 survey, based on listings in *Might's Toronto City Directory*, and also for the estimate of the Italian-origin population by the 1930s.

9 *Polyphony: The Bulletin of the Multicultural History Society of Ontario*, vol. 6 no. 1, 1984, "An Interview with Mary Caruso," p. 217.

10 Donina Lombardi-Hartig, "A Man Called Johnny Lombardi," *Italian Canadiana*, vol. 17, 2003, pp. 97-108, offers a good insight into Johnny Lombardi's life as remembered by his daughter.

11 Julius Molinaro, "Interned Italian Canadians Owed Apology," Toronto *Star*, 15 January 1990.

12 Franca Iacovetta, *Such Hardworking People: Italian Immigrants in Postwar Toronto*, Kingston and Montreal: McGill-Queen's University Press, 1992, in particular the excellent introductory chapters for an overview of post-Second World War Italian immigration to Canada and Toronto.

13 Fortunato Rao, *The Lucky Immigrant: The Public Life of Fortunato Rao*, Toronto: Multicultural History Society of Ontario and the Centre for Instructional Technology Press, 2001, pp. 31-35.

14 Cited in Angelo Principe, "Introduction: Two Years of Social Unrest in Toronto's Little Italy: 1960 & 1961," in Marino Toppan, *The Voice of Labour: A Life in Toronto's Construction Industry*, Toronto: (privately printed) c. 2003, pp. 1-33; see also Iacovetta, op. cit., for more discussion about the economic and other strategies pursued by "such hardworking people."

15 Rao, op. cit.

16 Angelo Principe and Gabriele Scardellato, interview with Giuseppe Simonetta, January 2000, author's collection, for a discussion about Toronto police attitudes toward immigrants who socialized in the streets. Simonetta, a former member of the Italian *Carabinieri* police force, who arrived in the early 1950s, was one of those who intervened with the local constabulary against the practice of asking people on the street to "disperse."

17 Gianni Grohovaz, "Toronto's Italian Press after the Second World War," *Polyphony: The Bulletin of the Multicultural History Society of Ontario*, vol. 4 no. 1, 1982, pp. 105-113.

18 *Corriere Canadese*, various advertisements found in the 9 December 1958 issue.

19 Toppan, op. cit., p. 44.

20 The role of impresario was also assumed by newcomers like Rocco Mastrangelo, who began his business life on College Street shortly after he arrived in 1957 to join his family. His career description is from an interview

Photos this page and opposite page: Vincenzo Pietropaolo

conducted by Angelo Principe and Gabriele Scardellato, January 2000, author's collection.

21 Gianni Grohovaz, "A Quest for Heritage: Piccolo Téatro Italiano," *Polyphony: The Bulletin of the Multicultural History Society of Ontario*, vol. 5 no. 2, 1983, pp. 47-55. Brandon Hall, or the Italo-Canadian Recreation Centre, located on Brandon Avenue, was the home for Toronto Italia's first community centre, eventually replaced by the present-day Columbus Centre.

22 Simonetta interview, January 2000.

23 Marchetto, op. cit.; Father Marchetto also notes that Italian-language services ended at St. Agnes in 1971.

24 Simonetta interview, January 2000.

25 Ibid.

26 Franc Sturino, "Contours of Postwar Italian Immigration to Toronto," *Polyphony: The Bulletin of the Multicultural History Society of Ontario*, vol. 6 no. 1, 1984, p. 130.

27 Robert Thomas Allen, "Portrait of Little Italy," *Maclean's*, 21 March 1964, p. 18.

28 Ibid., p. 44.

29 Mastrangelo interview, January 2000.

30 Ibid. Other bars in the neighbourhood that had preceded the Diplomatico included the Bar dello Sport, run for a time by Giuseppe Simonetta, the Capriccio, the Gatto Nero and so forth; see also Simonetta interview, 2000.

31 Interview by Gabriele Scardellato and Angelo Principe with Giovanna Luongo Manni, February 2000, author's collection.

32 Jason Hackworth and Josephine Rekers, "Ethnic Packaging and Gentrification: The Case of Four Neighborhoods in Toronto," *Urban Affairs Review*, vol. 41, 2005, pp. 211-236. The figures cited are based on the Little Italy boundaries of Bathurst Street and Dovercourt Road in the east and west respectively and Bloor and Dundas streets to the north and south.

33 Ibid., pp. 222-3.

34 Ibid., p. 222.

35 Celestino de Iuliis, "In My Backyard," in Caroline Morgan Di Giovanni, ed., *Italian Canadian Voices: An Anthology of Poetry and Prose (1946-1983)*, Oakville: Mosaic Press, 1984, p. 151.

Documenting the Heart of a Community

PHOTOGRAPHS BY VINCENZO PIETROPAOLO

RIGHT: The Easter procession
BELOW AND OPPOSITE PAGE: WORLD CUP FESTIVITIES

Bocce players in Bickford Park (1972).
Opposite page: Easter Procession is rained out, 1969.

Above: Porco Brothers butcher shop 1973.
Right: Bitondo Pizzeria
Opposite page: Bar Italia. Left to right: Nicola Seria, Bruno
Tassone and Carlo Croccolo during the filming of "Franco."

FILARMONICA LIRA BOM JESUS

OAKVILLE

ONTARIO

Early Portuguese Settlement in Toronto's Little Italy

DOMINGOS MARQUES & MANUELA MARUJO

Photo: Mark Fram (detail from a panorama)

Arms are my theme, and those matchless heroes
Who from Portugal's far western shores
By oceans where none had ventured
Voyaged to Taprobana and beyond,
Enduring hazards and assaults
Such as drew on more than human prowess
Among far distant peoples, to proclaim
A New Age and win undying fame

– LUÍS VAZ DE CAMÕES, opening of "The Lusiads"

On the northwest corner of College and Crawford stands a discreet statue of the most praised Portuguese poet, Luís Vaz de Camões. On the building's east wall, a mural of blue and white hand-painted tiles by Toronto ceramist Américo Ribeiro illustrates the memorable legend of Camões getting shipwrecked in 1559 at the mouth of the Mekong River on the poet's journey from China to India. Camões swam to shore using only one arm, saving his epic poem "The Lusiads" with the other. This poem is based on historically true events; it is a maritime odyssey where the discovery of India becomes the main theme, interlaced with the history of Portugal.

How did the statue of a 15th-century Portuguese poet end up in the heart of Toronto's Little Italy? It is known that Camões had a strong desire to rival the two greatest epic

writers up to that time, Homer and Virgil, as he proclaims in "The Lusiads": "Let us hear no more of Ulysses and Aeneas and their long journeying." Although some critics have considered Camões a great epic poet in the Western tradition, with Voltaire even naming him the Portuguese Virgil, the truth remains that there is no literary connection here. But there is a strong connection between Camões and the immigrants' experiences. Camões himself left the country as a young man to return 17 years later, after journeying through India, China and Africa. A great number of Portuguese who left their motherland identify with the poet's hardships and his journeying to foreign lands.

To the Portuguese, Camões also symbolizes the era of discoveries and expansion and Portugal's part in "opening

Antonio Sousa, owner of the first Portuguese restaurant in Toronto in the 1950s. PHOTO courtesy of Manuela Marujo and Domingos Marques

The brothers Martin and Isidro São José have had a front-row view of the evolution College Street has gone through in the past 30 years. They opened their family business, the São José Hardware store, at 556 College, back in 1971. "All this, across the street, around us, used to be doctors, lawyers," says Isidro, with a sweep of the hand. "Now? Only cafés!" PHOTO: Denis De Klerck

ABOVE LEFT: Banaboia Restaurant. PHOTO: Laurence Siegel

up" the modern world. So important is this epic poet to the Portuguese that the anniversary of his death - June 10 – became Portugal's National Day. And each year there are celebrations in every community around the world where Portuguese immigrants have settled. So it is only fitting that Toronto's Portuguese would also champion their hero poet with a statue of him next to their community centre, in a neighbourhood where Italians and Portuguese have been living side by side for decades. The June 10 Portugal Day celebrations have become the No. 1 community event for Toronto's Portuguese and their neighbours alike. And the corner of College and Crawford still provides the stage for a yearly public ceremony praising the virtues and values of a

people who, "desde a ocidental praia lusitana" (from the western coast of Portugal), began to track the ocean never sailed before by Europeans.

Portuguese and Italian immigrants of post-war Toronto settled in adjacent, and sometimes overlapping, residential areas. It is no surprise therefore that Toronto's Little Italy would also overlap with the Portuguese district. In the 1970s, the First Portuguese Canadian Club purchased the building at 722 College Street, moving its offices from the original quarters on Nassau Street, making this corner of Toronto the social and cultural hub of the Portuguese community during the formative years of the '70s and '80s.

There are many geographical, historical and social rea-

The Lisbon Bakery on Augusta Avenue, Kensington Market. PHOTO: Vincenzo Pietropaolo

Photo courtesy of Manuela Marujo and Domingos Marques

Américo Ribeiro

When Américo Ribeiro immigrated to Canada, he settled in Toronto's Portuguese community at first. He was a 25-year-old with a wife and daughter to support in Portugal, and so he started working odd jobs to raise money to send back home. But Ribeiro's talents and interests were ultimately in ceramics and ceramic painting, skills he started honing when he was only 14.

Today, Ribeiro's work is considered some of the best of its kind in Canada. It combines his own original designs with popular and traditional Portuguese patterns. Most distinguished among his work is his creation for the local Portuguese community centre and two historical ceramic murals he created for the Toronto City Hall Exhibition in 1993. Though he long ago moved out of the city's Portuguese community, into a new home and business in Mississauga, Ribeiro's creations show that he still remains closely connected to his roots.

The First Portuguese Canadian Club at Crawford and College (1991). Photo: Vincenzo Pietropaolo

sons to explain the early settlement of so many Portuguese immigrants around Toronto's Little Italy and, for that matter, around most "Little Italies" spread throughout North America. After all, North America emphasizes the individual and not the nuclear family, as the Italian and Portuguese societies do. The value systems of both ethnic groups, in particular the southern Italian and the Portuguese peasant from the interior and the Islands, were so similar that any psycho-sociological study of the one immigrant group could be applied almost in its entirety to the other. So Toronto Italians would become instrumental in facilitating the Portuguese newcomers' absorption into the city.

One could also argue that this assistance started even

before the Portuguese came to Canada. The discussions and negotiations between the Canadian and Portuguese immigration officials to open the Canadian borders to Portuguese immigrants were finalized only in December 1952, when the Canadian Minister of Immigration finally agreed that a small quota should be given to Portugal. As the immigration ministry attempted to include this experimental group in Canada's "1953 programme" – no quota had been previously allocated for the Portuguese – they had to borrow 200 spaces from the Italian allotment in order to select the first experimental group of "agriculturists and farmers" who arrived in Halifax, on May 13, aboard the Italian liner *Saturnia*.

Ironically, 20 years earlier, when Canadian authorities

ABOVE: Portuguese religious festivities.
Photo: Manuela Marujo and Domingos Marques.

RIGHT: St. Agnes Church. Photos Rick O'Brien

OPPOSITE: College Street has been an important meeting ground for World Cup soccer fans. Because of the large Portuguese population in Brazil, tradition dictates that if Portugal is eliminated, the Portuguese community on College will stand behind the Brazilian team, getting two chances to cheer for a win. Photo courtesy of Severino Manni

resisted various attempts by the Portuguese to immigrate to Canada, they had argued "the undesirability of Portuguese as immigrants" on the basis that the Portuguese were very much like the Italians, and so, "not particularly adaptable to farming conditions in Canada." Even in February 1953, as the selection of the Portuguese immigrants was being discussed between Laval Fortier, the Canadian Deputy Minister of Immigration, and G. Caldeira Coelho, the Chargé d'Affaires for Portugal, Italian immigrants were being used by Canada as scapegoats in the negotiations. In fact, Portuguese officials were interested primarily in resolving a severe "demographic problem" that existed in the Azores Islands. They wanted Canadians to take unskilled labourers and were arguing for the selection to be made in Ponta Delgada, chief city of São Miguel Island, Azores. The Canadians refused to consider it. They were prepared to take 100 farmers but also wanted some skilled *vinhateiros* (winegrowers), and only from the mainland and Madeira Island. The Canadian arguments were weak, referring again to the question of adaptability to the Canadian climate and the negative experience of Italian immigrants in Canada.

No real evidence of the so-called "negative experience" of Italians in Canada exists, only references by government officials and politicians quoted by some authors in various Canadian immigration studies. These comments are a result of a long-standing myth created, in part, by the immigration policies of one of the most celebrated figures in Canadian immigration history, Clifford Sifton.

Sifton, a minister in Wilfrid Laurier's government elected in 1896, launched an aggressive campaign to recruit agricultural immigration for settlement of the Canadian West. Not finding enough British or Americans interested, he preferred northern to southern Europeans and considered Italians ill-fitted for pioneering. Thousands of Italians nevertheless came to Canada from Italy and from the "Little Italies" of the American east coast in those years. Most were peasants or sharecroppers, small landowners and rural day labourers, unable to speak English on arrival from the impoverished southern regions of Italy where they had wrested a living from a harsh environment and struggled against an exploitative socio-economic order.

After working for the summer in Canada, many returned home to contribute their savings toward the upkeep of their southern Italian villages and collect dowries for sisters and daughters. Those who did not make it back to Italy wintered in the railhead cities, notably Montreal. When railway work was succeeded by labouring jobs for inter-urban and street railways, more Italians decided to stay in the cities. Instead of returning to Italy, young men sent for their wives or other relatives, initiating a process of chain migration that was reaching a peak when the Portuguese arrived in 1953. Those who returned to Italy may have contributed to the perception that they could not adapt to the country, but that was obviously not the case. Was this the so-called "negative experience of the Italians" then? They certainly adapted like everyone else to the Canadian climate and all other obstacles.

The so-called negative experience of Italian immigrants in Canada was only a red herring. However, it did not stop Canadian officials from attempting to use it in their arguments with Portugal while negotiating the opening of their borders to Portuguese immigrants.

In a five-page letter sent urgently and confidentially to the Portuguese Foreign Affairs Minister on February 25, 1953, the Portuguese Chargé d'Affaires in Ottawa wrote:

The Canadian officials once more insisted on the fact that, what they had agreed this year with the Portuguese immigrants was an experiment only. And if it provided good results, then Canada would look at the Portuguese case in a larger framework. They emphasized the loss of credibility among Canadians relative to the Latin immigrants, due to previous experiences [referring to the Italian immigration] and the political aspect of admitting to Canada large Catholic groups which could only be considered if they proved to be worthwhile as a result of their character and work ethic.

A Tale of Two Silvas

Mario Silva

Thirty years after immigrating here from Portugal with his family, Mario Silva did something in 2006 that made Canadian history. He ran in the federal election, won his riding and became this country's first Portuguese-Canadian Member of Parliament.

Silva lived, grew up and went to school in his Davenport riding, and has always been involved in the community. Before his big win at the federal level, Silva was a city councillor and even served as acting mayor. But it was his commitment to helping newcomers through their arrival and transition into Canadian society – something he had to face himself as a kid – that helped him gain popularity locally.

Silva has even co-authored a collection of personal stories from new immigrants entitled Fabric of a Nation: Stories of the Journey to Canada.

Martin Silva

For years, Toronto's Portuguese woke up to one man's voice every morning. Speaking through the radio, bright and early each day for over 20 years, was the unmistakable voice of Martin Silva.

Silva, who was born in Portugal, came to Canada in 1968 and made his name at CHIN Radio quickly. His popularity in the Portuguese community soared in the 1970s and '80s thanks to two morning shows: Ecos De Portugal and Wake Up Portuguese Style.

Over the years, Silva's personality has proven to be equally popular outside of radio land; he was a city councillor for nine years, and has also served as a union representative.

Though Silva has gone back and forth between his political stints and radio gigs, wherever he is, he has always been a vocal advocate for the Portuguese community in Toronto, whether it be against deportation of Portuguese workers or for Portuguese language programming on airwaves.

Photo: Vincenzo Pietropaolo

In the end, though, the Italians came and so did the Portuguese, including men from the Azores, opening the way to all other "warm blooded Latinos."

The first handfuls of Portuguese immigrants arrived in Toronto during the summer of 1953. Some of these "pioneers," like Antonio Sousa, are still around to tell you the heartbreaking stories of their first battles and the culture shock of the daily struggle of life:

> I took the train from Halifax to Montreal, and from Montreal on to Toronto, where I had to stay awaiting orders for two or three days. I found accommodation in a small guesthouse on Bay and Charles Street for three dollars a day. I went out to a restaurant on the corner of Dundas Street for my meals. One morning, as I was sitting on a stool by the bar, there sat next to me a man who was dirty black from the coal sacks it was his job to deliver. I was shocked. I immediately went into my room and wrote to my wife: "I am still without a job, but I have decided this very minute that I am going to stay in Canada. If a man who delivers coal can sit down in a nice restaurant next to a man dressed in a suit and tie, then this is the country for me."
>
> There were three or four Portuguese families in Toronto in 1953 when I left for Labrador. But when I got back nine months later, there were already many more. Kensington Market looked

Photos courtesy of Domingos Marques and Manuela Marujo

Photo: Tony Azevedo

like a market back home, all the merchandise out on the streets in full view of everybody. Beans and rice were sold exactly the same way as they would be in Portugal. If you wanted to buy fruit, for example, you selected your own, then went and paid for it.

The City of Toronto was going through a significant change in the makeup of its population. The great wave of migration in the early 1900s, made up of Jews, Italians, as well as immigrants from eastern Europe, had already established many ethnic settlements in Toronto. Unlike the other, English-speaking immigrants, these were considered "foreigners," as one can see from a 1927 survey, commissioned by the Toronto Public Library board of the College Street Library district to assess its users' needs. It read:

The southern part of our district is populated by foreigners. Statistics of the proportion of races in the district we found impossible to get. From the neighbourhood workers we learned that the district known as the Ward which is bound by College, Yonge, Queen and University, has about 55% Jewish population, 15% Italian, and the rest ... other nationalities.

With the city no longer inhabited by a majority of "British stock," officials would gradually change their attitude toward ethnicity and the immigrants of non-British descent, learning in the process a great lesson about tolerance and the rest of the world. The Portuguese would have encountered

a very different reception upon their arrival if those ethnic settlements, in particular the Italians, had not been there to serve them as halfway houses between old-country and Canadian ways.

When the first Portuguese immigrants began arriving in Toronto, they settled around Kensington Market, with their stores spilling over the sidewalks. Chickens could be bought, still alive, from cages, and fresh-fruit stores and vegetable stands were there in abundance. A tourist's romantic image was created for this neighbourhood, as the Portuguese changed Kensington Market's landscape by painting the old and decrepit Victorian houses in a full array of bright colours, and by putting their vegetable gardens in front, mixing in a profusion of purple hydrangeas or red dahlias. They also favoured adorning their patios, as a sign of their devotion, with religious statuary to Our Lady of Fatima, the Holy Family. In Azorean homes appeared the image of "*Senhor Santo Cristo*" (Christ of the Miracles). Augusta Avenue, a name with a Portuguese ring to it, became "*Rua Augusta,*" lined with produce stalls, bakeries and fish stores.

For decades, Antonio Sousa's restaurant, at the corner of Nassau and Bellevue, became a meeting place for newcomers: they would arrive directly from the airport and search there for a place to stay, a first job or an old friend. "*Rua Augusta*" was the place to shop, to socialize, to feel more at home, but it became too small a place to accommodate the large numbers of immigrants who invaded Toronto in a few short years. Gradually the community spread westward along both

College and Dundas toward Ossington Avenue, and northward to Bloor Street, living side by side with the Italians and following them around Bellwoods Park, which today is still referred to by the Portuguese as "*Parque dos Italianos*" (the Italian Park).

In the early 1960s, as family reunification of the first wave of immigrants was taking place, two new types of immigrant began arriving from Portugal: the more skilled technician and the white-collar worker with at least secondary school education. They had learned either basic English or French before leaving home or quickly managed to pick up the language through night school in Toronto. Upon their arrival in Toronto, these new immigrants quickly saw business opportunities, and many entrepreneurs set up shop as bakers, restaurateurs, hairstylists, photographers and travel agents, all catering mainly to other Portuguese.

From Augusta Avenue westward, many businesses and services flourished on College, such as Lisbon Service Station, Banco Fonsecas & Burnay, Easy Driving School, Orbit Furniture and many others that have since moved on. Some entrepreneurs, like Frank Silva, who started the Imperio Travel Agency on College just west of Augusta, are still in business more than three decades later, albeit a bit further west and now on Dundas instead. Others, like Frank Alvarez, who was a business partner at Imperio Restaurant next to the travel agency of the same name, went on to develop a catering business before entering radio, television and other media. Today, following in the footsteps of his for-

LEFT: Trinity Bellwoods Park was known to the Portuguese as "the park of the Italians" when they began to settle west of Kensington Market in the 1960s. This photo shows the June 10 Portugal Day celebration in 1988, which featured members of a folkloric group from Castelo de Neiva, Portugal. Photo: Martin Silva.

mer boss and role model, Johnny Lombardi of CHIN, Alvarez owns and runs his own multicultural radio station – CIRV Radio, serving the Portuguese community as well as various ethnic communities. Other entrepreneurs, like Bento de São José, who, for many years, operated a gas station at the corner of College and Bathurst, would go on to expand throughout the city. Others still – like Bento's brother, Isidro de São José, at São José Hardware on College at Euclid – would continue to serve Little Italy's residents.

By 1965, with each wave of sponsored relatives, the Portuguese community was expanding and already counting in excess of 10,000 new immigrants. As soon as they were able to, they purchased houses – for back in their homeland, every family had its own home. As the community expanded from the Kensington Market area, they moved westward through Dundas and College streets – the two main arteries carrying the lifeblood of the community around Toronto's Little Italy, which was gradually infiltrated by the Portuguese newcomers. The initial area of Portuguese concentration after Kensington and Alexander Park was the area west of Bathurst along College to Dovercourt Road, and northward to Bloor Street. They looked for houses where costs were lower and which the family could renovate. Typically they would paint the outside of the house in the bright colours familiar in the homeland. When a house was to undergo major renovations, a work party of relatives and friends would be called to assist on weekends. Traditionally, beer or homemade wine was served and a large meal cooked by the women, and the

day would end in a party atmosphere. Those who helped would feel free, in turn, to call later for assistance when they had a similar project underway.

Social activities and social services for the newcomers in Toronto were initially provided by St. Christopher House, and the Portuguese Consulate, and soon after by St. Mary's Church on Bathurst at Adelaide. This parish would become, for many years, the centre of much community activity in the life of the Portuguese community.

Several priests provided religious services at St. Mary's from 1956 until 1966, when Father Alberto Cunha took over the parish. It was during his time that the church became the most active centre of community activity, next to the First Portuguese Canadian Club. In addition to the religious services, there was a permanent community centre offering social assistance and services such as interpreting, crisis intervention, employment, and social and recreation activities for youth.

Soon after Father Cunha arrived at St. Mary's, the procession of Senhor Santo Cristo became the largest Portuguese Catholic religious ceremony in North America. The original Christ of the Miracles statue is housed in a chapel of Ponta Delgada, the capital of São Miguel Island, Azores. In Toronto, a successful Azorean entertainer, Mariano Rego, gave St. Mary's an image of Christ of the Miracles, which each year is carried in the procession. Roman Catholicism was and still is an integral component of Portuguese traditions because of a long national history in which no other religion had a

large number of followers. Community picnics, fairs, dances and opportunities to meet old acquaintances and friends are strongly associated with religious festivals. As the community developed and moved westward, another parish was set up at St. Agnes in 1970, to serve the many thousands who had settled in the College Street Little Italy area. A very popular celebration by the parishioners of St. Agnes is Senhor da Pedra (Lord of the Stone), a devotion celebrated in early August and especially associated with the town of Vila Franca do Campo, in São Miguel island.

In the 1970s, after the more basic needs of the immigrants had been met, the community was finally ready to look around and outward and began to build its own institutions. This allowed the immigrants to participate and become more active in the larger urban community. An event that contributed significantly to this change took place in 1974 in the homeland. On April 25, a bloodless coup by the armed forces ended almost 50 years of dictatorship and brought about many significant changes in Portuguese society. Although many Toronto Portuguese were mere spectators of the events and changes, one can use this date to mark the beginning of a new era in the community.

In the early '70s, thousands of young men evaded military service. Some came to Canada as visitors and then took advantage of laws that allowed them to obtain landed immigrant status. As a result of Canadian immigration policy, a flow of more skilled and better-educated immigrants had started to arrive, and by 1976, the Portuguese population

Above: Soccer fans at World Cup on College.
Photo: Francis Crescia

Left: Liga Luso Canadiana (1968)
Photo courtesy of Manuela Marujo and Domingos Marques

of Toronto alone had reached 92,000. They were served by several newspapers: *Correio Português*, *Comunidade* and *Jornal Açoriano* (others, like *Novo Mundo* and *Jornal Português*, had already folded).Radio programming in Portuguese was on the air every afternoon through CHIN, as well as daily programming through cable: *Rádio Clube Português* and *Asas do Atlântico*. The community could also watch television in its language through Global Television Network on weekends with *Festival Português,* and *Portugal de Hoje* on Citytv, daily.

Although the immigrants had always shown a keen interest in nurturing their cultural and religious beliefs with the formation of many associations and clubs, it was after the democratic revolution of April 25, 1974, that the community came of age.

Many regionally based clubs were organized and expanded. The First Portuguese Canadian Club (FPCC), a focal point for recreational, cultural and educational activities, gained wide recognition when it moved into the middle of Little Italy, becoming the social and cultural centre as well as the meeting place for the Portuguese community in the '70s and '80s.

When telling the story of the Portuguese immigrants in Toronto, one cannot separate it from the FPCC, their first social-cultural organization, founded in September 1956, just three years after the arrival of the first contingent of Portuguese immigrants. "The First," as it is commonly known in the community, has touched the lives of many people – children, youth, men and women and seniors. Recreation, education, sports, politics and art all appear on the many pages written in its history. In 1964, the First opened its "school" with D. Branca Gomes and has continued to deliver after-school Portuguese language classes to thousands of children and youngsters. In the world of sports, its soccer team joined the National Soccer League, twice winning the Ontario championship, which promoted the love of the sport among young and old. One of its soccer players, the multi-talented Armando Costa of Rilhas, would go on to coach overseas, as well as develop a singing career. Cyclists from the club have represented Canada at the Olympics

Tomás Ferreira

To say Tomás Ferreira is one of the busiest and most tireless workers in the Portuguese community would be making an understatement about the good doctor. For all the work he has done since immigrating to Canada and opening his family practice here in the 1970s, Ferreira would best be acknowledged with the Mr. Portugal title.

It wouldn't be the first prestigious title he has held – Ferreira currently serves as president of the Portuguese Canadian National Congress, the First Portuguese Canadian Cultural Centre, the Portuguese Canadian Credit Union and the Council of Communities, which advises the Portuguese government on issues related to its citizens abroad.

Ferreira has volunteered for countless other Portuguese organizations and was instrumental in founding the Kensington Clinic, which brought alcohol and drug addiction treatment services to the Portuguese community in its own language.

Besides his consistent presence in the community, Ferreira has also lent his voice and pen to the people here for many years – he writes a column for The Voice newspaper and he co-hosts a weekly health program on CHIN Radio that has been running uninterrupted since it first went on air in 1988.

Elsewhere, Ferreira has also worked with Amnesty International and was a founding member of the Canadian Centre for Victims of Torture.

Ask anyone in the Portuguese community and they will tell you that Dr. Ferreira's work in and for the community is unmatched. The Portuguese government awarded him a Medal of Merit for his efforts in the 1980s.

Photo: Rick O'Brien

and Commonwealth Games. And hockey, Canada's national sport, would also thrive in the organization under the leadership of Mario Corte-Real. Dozens of trophies are still proudly displayed in the First. Folk dance groups, fado singers, theatre performers, painters and other artists have had their debuts in the club's halls. The club members' support of the artists has given singers like Shawn Desmond, Michelle Tavares and Catarina Cardeal the push they needed to pursue their careers in mainstream society.

The club has since lost much of its importance as a social meeting point, as the community has moved north and to other parts of Toronto, as well as to Mississauga and southwestern Ontario, but it still houses the offices of the First, later renamed the First Portuguese Canadian Cultural Centre, as well as the Alliance of Portuguese Clubs and Associations of Ontario, the Federation of Portuguese Canadian Business and Professionals and the Pioneers' Gallery, a collection of artifacts, books and documents associated with the first wave of Portuguese immigration.

Further west at Dovercourt and College was another important community centre: the West End YMCA. John Medeiros, its outreach worker in charge of the Portuguese department in the 1970s, summarizes its relevance:

In the 1970s the West End Y was desperately looking for someone to do outreach work with Portuguese youth. The media at the time reported some tension among different youth groups. A small group of Portuguese youth was becoming a concern for

West End YMCA.

the parents and the police. They were hanging out with nothing to do in the parks and billiard halls, and sometimes getting into trouble. The question was how to get them involved in more acceptable and meaningful activities.

Learning English was a major concern, and so was the lack of basic information about Canadian society. There was a need to develop an organizing structure that would lead and advocate for programs to address the different needs of the community. To give form to the organization, I recruited a group of enthusiastic youth among senior high school and university students and founded the Portuguese Development Committee. This group of young men and women would meet regularly to generate ideas to start meaningful programs in the community. Out of their initiatives grew programs such as bilingual ESL classes for adults, summer camps for children with Portuguese language instruction and culture as the main focus, a newsletter – Informações – that later became the Portuguese community newspaper Comunidade *and a cable TV program. There were several discussion forums on issues related to political participation. Many reports were written, and one manual for community organizations, called* Programming for Participation. *The need to preserve the oral history of the first Portuguese immigrants led to development of a research project and the publication of the book* Portuguese Immigrants: 25 Years in Canada, *in collaboration with Domingos Marques.*

Many of the West End Y's initiatives were seminal, setting the stage for a major growth in leadership and the flourish-

RIGHT: Portuguese community leaders gather at Chiado Restaurant. Virgilio Piris (left), Amilcor Jacinto, Leo Pereira, Frank Alvarez, Armindo Silva.

ing of new Portuguese community organizational structures and networks. Portuguese Free Interpreting Services also came into existence under the leadership of St. Christopher's House. Soon after, other organizations catering to the social needs of the community, such as Portuguese Interagency Network, were created.

Upon their arrival in a foreign country and a city still very much "British," it is not surprising that the Portuguese flocked to Toronto's Little Italy area. After all, Italians looked familiar and possessed habits and values forged in similar rural peasant economies in southern Europe. When the Portuguese men brought their wives and children to Canada and had to rent or buy a house, an Italian neighbourhood made a better fit than any other group. Italian and Portuguese had a similar linguistic structure. They also shared the family culture of work, where each person was expected to sacrifice individual needs and aspirations to contribute to the famiy's survival. The resemblance and experiences extended into the bakeries, the Catholic churches, the shops, the network of trades, leisure activities and even the annual celebrations held in honour of their patron saints.

Their arrival in Canada's largest city was part of a larger diaspora that saw millions of both Portuguese and Italians migrate temporarily or permanently to countries in Europe, the Americas and elsewhere around the world. In both cases, emigration had been a popular response to economic problems in their home countries. And they also shared a tradition of romance languages, fascist regimes and Catholic religion with traditional supports of family, kin and *paesani* alike. So much so that until the 1970s, among the general population of Toronto, including the academics, the Portuguese were often mistakenly thought of as Italians.

Eventually the numbers of the Portuguese grew significantly, the community had integrated into mainstream society, and their impact on the construction and development of the city at all levels was recognized. The Portuguese, like the Italians, came to be referred to by political officials as "honest, hard-working immigrants" who have contributed so much to the building of Canada and its cities. In particular, during visits of Portuguese officials, the Portuguese immigrants are praised as "nation builders." According to scholars like Franca Iacovetta, referring to the Italians, this self-image of "honest, hard-working immigrant" creates "an important psychological defense against their low position on the city's occupational ladder."

Today, after 50 years in Canada, the almost half-million Portuguese Canadians remain with a strong sense of their history, a sound appreciation of their country's historic role in the shaping of the modern world that the era of the Discoveries represented. There remain many battles to further progress in the Canadian political and corporate world. The Italians arrived first and have slowly conquered a leading place in Canadian society. Many Portuguese in the community see the Italians as the model to emulate, and they fully expect to have similar outcomes.

Frank Alvarez

Frank Alvarez, founder of the multicultural radio station 88.9 CIRV FM, is an entrepreneur at heart. Since he immigrated here in 1967, his ventures have contributed not only to the Portuguese community but also to the larger multicultural mosaic in Canada.

In the 1970s, the former co-owner of Imperio Restaurant on College Street found his true calling in ethnic media. After starting as a part-time announcer for local Portuguese radio and television, Alvarez went on to produce Portuguese programming for Metro Cable Television and then Global TV.

Then, in 1986, things really took off. Alvarez's CIRV Radio made its first broadcast and the rest is history. Now, Alvarez's "family station" is considered the most popular station among Portuguese listeners in the Toronto area. With over 60 hours a week of Portuguese programming on its airwaves, that's not hard to imagine.

Alvarez's latest venture, Festival Portuguese TV, is already making waves as Canada's first and only 24-hour Portuguese digital channel.

In 1998, Alvarez received a special honour of merit from the Portuguese president to acknowledge his dedication to the Portuguese community in Canada.

An immigrant family arrives in Toronto (1910). Photo: TA

Traces Left Behind

The "Other" Communities of College Street

GIULIANA COLALILLO

The traces left behind along College Street by the many immigrant groups who arrived in Toronto, from when it was known as "Muddy York" to our present-day cosmopolitan city, are sometimes faint, washed away by time and progress; at other times the traces are more firmly etched in the streets, houses, buildings and churches that these settlers made their own. Initially crowded into reception areas, the most infamous and largest known as the Ward, the early immigrants and their offspring began to scatter throughout the city. College Street, especially toward the east end, became both a destination and point of departure for those men, women and children. Whether arriving on ships or on airplanes, in the end, all the newcomers shared the dream of finding "*America*," the proverbial Promised Land. For many, the journey in this new land started on College Street.

The evolution and transformation of College Street during the 20th century mirrors the changes that occurred throughout the City of Toronto as it left behind its solidly Anglo-Saxon beginnings to become one of the most ethnically diverse cities in the world. In addition to the larger immigrant groups who are commonly identified with College Street today – the Jews, Italians and Portuguese – other immigrant groups have also left a part of their history on this street. Though they may serve a different purpose or population, if you stand in front of the older houses, buildings and churches that line College and the surrounding avenues and boulevards, it is easy to imagine the multiplicity of voices and languages spoken by their former occupants.

Contours of early College Street

When the boundaries of Toronto extended west only to Dufferin Street and north to Bloor, there were few carriage paths that crossed east-west along the 100-acre north-south tracts of land that ran from Queen Street to Bloor. As these strips of land, referred to as "park lots," were subdivided by the owners and their inheritors, the contours of College Street and its environs began to take shape. Roads began to be carved as sections of the land were subdivided, and were named after extended family members of the original Anglo-Saxon owners. The name of College Street itself derives from King's College – the precursor to the University of Toronto – which stood on the site of today's Ontario Legislature buildings.

An early plan for College Street called for it to be a wide boulevard of mansions for the city's elite. For a while, graceful estates dotted the area south of College, stretching from Yonge to Spadina; these large houses were nestled in a restful mixture of woods and farmland at the outskirts of the city proper and had names such as Belle Vue, Willows and the Hall, built by Sir Casimir Gzowski, a Polish nobleman and immigrant to the city. But as the end of the century approached, this idyllic setting gave way to development, and when College Street was extended in the 1870s, it took on the characteristics of a more typical Toronto street. As the built-up area of College crept west past Spadina, housing, churches and schools were constructed. Indeed, most of the residential housing on either side of College as far west as

Bathurst was built or developed in the building boom of the 1880s. The area immediately surrounding Spadina, south of College, became populated with prosperous, middle-class families who moved into large, architect-designed homes. Up to 1891, residents could ride up Spadina, along College to Bathurst Street on the horse-drawn streetcars of the privately owned Toronto Street Railway Company. And soon after the turn of the century, a new electric streetcar service was introduced by the Toronto Railway Line, another privately owned company that was later taken over by the city's new public transit commission.

Like most of the city at the time, College had a distinctively British character. These new residents quickly built parish churches, which became the nerve centres of their community. Joining St. Stephen-in-the-Fields (at Bellevue), the first church built west of Spadina in 1858, were newer churches. College Street Presbyterian, built in 1884-5 at the northwest corner of Bathurst and College, is now College Street United Church (surrounded by the College Condominiums complex). College Street Baptist, now the Portuguese Seventh-Day Adventist Church, was constructed in 1888 at the northwest corner of Palmerston and College. It was the larger and newer building for the Baptist congregation who moved from their smaller church not far away at 410 College – a structure that still survives as St. George Lutheran Church. Schools were built: Bathurst Street School (1872), later renamed King Edward, and in 1888, Lord Lansdowne on Spadina Crescent. And, pre-dating the destructive 1904 Great

Babysitter in the Ward (1912). Photo: TA

Toronto Fire, which gutted most of downtown Toronto, was No. 8 Hose Station at College and Bellevue, built in 1878. Following a devastating fire of its own in 1972, the fire station was completely rebuilt so that its clock tower still dominates the surrounding area.

The Ward: an immigrant reception area

At the beginning of the 20th century, the area around College and University Avenue changed dramatically, as the estates were torn down or put to other uses. Upper-middle-class Anglo-Saxons moved to enclaves on Euclid Avenue and Palmerston Boulevard, where architect-designed houses were built to reflect the status and wealth of the new owners.

College Street became lined with commercial buildings. By 1911, the City of Toronto boasted a sizable number of immigrants from different parts of Europe and the Russian Pale. Many were escaping repressive empires and dire poverty. The area west of Yonge and south of College Street became a key immigrant reception area from 1880 onward, with its focal centre in the north and central part of St. John's Ward, commonly referred to as "the Ward." Within the confines of this densely populated area, roughly bounded by College Street to the north, Queen Street to the south, Yonge Street on the east and University Avenue on the west, a mixture of ethnic groups lived. Jews from eastern Europe lived side by side with Italians from rural regions of the south. Closer to Queen

LEFT: Children in the Ward (1908). Photo: TA
ABOVE: Napping in the Ward (1909). Photo: TA

Street, Poles, Finns, Ukrainians and Chinese newcomers were interspersed among the Jewish majority.

Resembling a railway shantytown more than the tenement slums typical of New York City immigrant neighbourhoods, the living conditions and overcrowding of the Ward became a cause for concern and an eyesore. The absentee landlords did little to make their properties more habitable. As land values skyrocketed, the area became a developer's dream. Armed with a 1911 report from the city's Medical Officer of Health, obliteration of the Ward and the dispersal of the foreigners who lived there became the logical course of action for the city's guardians. The Ward's dilapidated housing was cleared away to make space for the city's new hospital wards.

The hospital district

It is certainly the case that College Street has an overabundance of hospitals in its confines. There are many scientific firsts in the string of world-class hospitals that today line University Avenue – Toronto Hospital, Mount Sinai, the Hospital for Sick Children, Princess Margaret – or further west at Toronto Western Hospital on Bathurst Street south of College. Perhaps the stage was set even before the turn of the century, when the area first hosted a number of specialized hospitals serving the College Street neighbourhoods.

The care of children became the focus for a group of women who started what was to become the world-renowned Hospital for Sick Children by renting a house and setting

up six cots in 1875. The Victorian Hospital for Sick Children moved into its own building on College and Elizabeth Street in 1891, where it remained for over 60 years. The building, newly refurbished, is now home to Canadian Blood Services, formerly known as the Canadian Red Cross.

Further west, the precursor of the Toronto Western Hospital was established in 1894 when several west-end doctors established a hospital for that part of the city. The Western Free Dispensary, an outpatient clinic for needy patients, was located first on Bathurst, then on Euclid. Later, a ward for 30 patients was opened in a double house on Manning Avenue. Eventually the hospital occupied its current location by taking over the Willows estate on the east side of Bathurst, south of Nassau. Toronto Western Hospital has distinguished itself in the treatment and care of the many immigrant groups in the neighbourhood. It has also

provided jobs for many of the immigrants and their children: where the immigrant parents were hired to clean the wards and work in the kitchen, the children may now be found staffing offices or providing professional care as health workers.

One hospital in the area that did not survive into the 21st century started as the first surgical hospital for women in the city around 1889 on Major Street, just north of College. Patients in St. John's Hospital for Women were tended by an Anglican order of nuns. For over 60 years, the care facility expanded and flourished. Even after it was sold to four doctors, the Raxlen brothers, in 1953 and renamed Doctors Hospital, it continued to grow, becoming the largest privately owned acute care facility in Canada when a 10-storey tower was added in 1958. It was distinguished by the care it gave to the needs of the local community and Toronto's growing multi-

cultural population, providing medical services in a variety of languages even after it became a public general hospital in 1969. The community successfully lobbied to keep the hospital open after plans to close it down were announced in 1976. However, similar arguments about the distinctive character of the hospital and the community it served were not successful in the '90s: the doors of Doctors Hospital closed forever in 1997, and the building was torn down to make way for Kensington Gardens, a long-term care facility that opened in 2003. Happily, Kensington Gardens carries on in the spirit of Doctors Hospital, with a mandate to serve and reflect the multicultural community that surrounds it.

Settlement houses to help the immigrant community
Another mainstay of the area from the turn of the century – albeit in a more culturally sensitive and updated fashion

A protest at the Doctor's Hospital.

Photos this page: Vincenzo Pietropaolo

Mandarin class at St. David's Catholic School; part of a St. Stephen's Community House program (2005).

Schoolchildren at the Dewson Street Public School.

Chinese seniors rehearsing a dance routine at the Senior Activities Centre of St. Stephen's Community House on College Street (2005).

– are the services offered by settlement houses. Started in Britain as a broad attempt to preserve human values in an urban and industrial age, the settlement movement took on a character of its own when it crossed the ocean. In Toronto, its goal was to work with the poor immigrant newcomers with the intent of alleviating some of the urban ills caused by rapid industrialization and increasing immigration. So it was that the Presbyterian Church of Canada established St. Christopher House in 1912, locating it on Wales Avenue in the Kensington Market area. The workers, often middle-class women who were essentially pioneer social workers, offered literacy classes, ran social clubs, facilitated baby clinics and organized athletic clubs. Today St. Christopher's is a non-sectarian institution that serves a wide number of immigrant and non-immigrant groups in Toronto's downtown core.

The Anglican Diocese of Toronto also operated a mission in the area, occupying a large house that had been built for the first minister of nearby College Street Presbyterian Church. The Nathanael Institute was established to work among the Jews in the neighbourhood, with the express goal of converting them to Christianity. It offered night-school English classes, dispensary, home and hospital visits, mothers' meetings, Sunday school, sewing classes and also relief and job placement. The institute survived until the mid-1950s, although its success at conversion was very limited. Some years later, in 1962, the Anglican Diocese established

St. Stephen's Community House in the same building to offer support to the youth living in the College and Spadina areas. By 1964, English classes for new immigrants were available, as well as counselling, job placement services, and electronics and woodworking workshops for youth. St. Stephen's Community House has been an independent, incorporated, not-for-profit charitable organization since 1974, offering an even wider assortment of services to the community. St. Stephen's recently expanded its services to a renovated building on Augusta Avenue in Kensington Market and now includes a soup kitchen and accommodations for homeless men.

Westward bound

With the dismantling of the Ward, an increasing number of residents moved west, settling in the area between Spadina and Bathurst, and further to Clinton and Grace streets; others joined their compatriots in the Junction, where housing was also affordable and close to work. The Jewish community established its presence east of Spadina in a *shtetl*-like environment: 35,000 lived in and around Kensington by the 1920s, worshipping in over 30 local synagogues. The Jewish market, a.k.a. Kensington Market, was born: a vibrant commercial area that has grown and changed to provide goods and services to many ethnic groups, then as now. The smaller number of Italian immigrants settled around

College and Dundas streets, congregating around St. Agnes Church, making it the second Italian parish in Toronto, after Our Lady of Mount Carmel on Dundas West. For a time, in addition to the Jews and Italians, this western part of College Street had a presence of Hungarians, Latvians, Lithuanians, Poles and even Irish immigrants.

The Western District Orange Hall

As the immigrants moved west along College Street, buildings that had served the cultural and religious interests of the Protestant population came under different uses. One example is the Western District Orange Hall, at the corner of College and Euclid. Used as a meeting place for members of the Orange Order, a Protestant Irish society established in the 18th century to maintain Protestant ascendancy in Ireland, it was the venue for banquets honouring illustrious Orangemen such as H. Hocken, a trade unionist, journalist, mayor of Toronto and MPP for the riding of West Toronto. From 1913 to 1915, the building was turned over to the Dewi Sant Welsh United Church. The Welsh Church eventually left to take over the Christian Worker's Church at 54 Clinton Street, where it remained for over 40 years, until 1957. Orange Hall later became a banquet hall and now houses some of the first condominiums in the neighbourhood, replete with a trendy café on the first floor at the front of the building.

OUTSTANDING CANDIDATE

Elect **Stan GRIZZLE**

Stanley G. Grizzle

Stanley G. Grizzle has made a life and career out of doing more than what was expected of him. At 22, he started as a railway porter, became a labour activist and then went on to become a decorated war veteran, union president, civil rights activist and, now, retired citizenship judge at the age of 88.

Grizzle was born in Toronto in 1918, seven years after his parents immigrated to Canada from Jamaica. The entrenched racism Grizzle saw in his own city and at his first real job would change his life. When he started at the Canadian Pacific Rail, most all of his fellow porters were black. They were allowed to sleep only three or four hours a night, Grizzle says, and they ate meals of leftover food from passengers while separated from white employees by a curtain. When he became one of the chief founders of Toronto's local of the Brotherhood of Sleeping Car Porters union, he knew they had to work together to fight for their rights—and not just over the details of their jobs, but more important, around the unspoken civil rights issues underneath. He became the local's president shortly after returning from Europe at the end of the Second World War.

In the 1950s, Grizzle got involved in the civil rights movement that was emerging in this country, working with the city's Joint Labour Committee to Combat Racial Intolerance. He later went on to work for the Ontario Labour Relations Board, and in 1978 was appointed a Canadian Citizenship Court Judge.

In recognition of his work, Grizzle received the Order of Ontario in 1990 and then the Order of Canada five years later.

Harry Gairey and fellow CPR porters. Photo: TPL

Irish

There is also a scant reference to a group of destitute Irish who made Mansfield Avenue their home for a time around the turn of the century. It may be that this was a minor area of Irish Catholic concentration generally labelled Irish Town. For the most part, Irish clusters in Toronto were found by the waterfront and in the area of the Don Basin; they were often referred to as Slab Town, Paddy Town or Cork Town, and later Cabbagetown in the east, and Claretown, as the area around Bathurst and Queen was known around 1850.

The contribution of Irish Catholics to the institutional structure of the city is very significant. We owe the building of St. Michael's Cathedral, St. Patrick's Church and many other Roman Catholic churches in the city to the Irish Catholic population: from 1850 to 1914, 14 Roman Catholic churches were constructed in the city, in each case to serve the needs of growing areas of Irish Catholic concentration. Likewise, institutions such as St. Michael's High School, St. Michael's College of the University of Toronto and St. Michael's Hospital have their roots in the Irish Catholic's need to create institutions that would serve his cultural and religious beliefs. Needless to say, other Catholic immigrants availed themselves of these institutions and felt more comfortable in the religious and educational milieus of College Street and its environs as a result of the struggles and successes of the Irish Catholics.

Toronto General Hospital (circa 1910s). Photo: TPL

Harry Gairey

Harry Gairey once knew most every black family in Toronto. Later in his life, the tables would turn – Gairey would be the one most every black family knew and looked up to. They would even come to have an affectionate nickname for him: Grand Old Man.

Gairey was admired for his love and compassion for the people around him. And what fight he had inside of him to do what was best for his people; Gairey can be counted as one of Toronto's earliest civil rights activists. Aside from his work challenging federal immigration laws, he was the man who forced this city to take a stance against racial discrimination. It had been a simple matter of pure paternal instinct for Gairey. His son was told he couldn't go into a local ice rink because he was "coloured," so Gairey went directly to City Hall to straighten things out. The confrontation was all over the papers the next day. City Council responded with a historic anti-discrimination ordinance and Gairey was on his way.

Gairey later co-founded both the Negro Citizenship Association and the West Indian Federation Club on Brunswick Avenue. After the WIF Club had to close shop when a fire gutted the building they were in, Gairey said that he would walk down the street and people would stop him and say "Mr. Gairey, when are we going to open another WIF Club? Nothing like the WIF."

For his efforts, he was given the National Black Coalition Community Award in 1973 and an Order of Distinction from the Jamaican government in 1977. The Grand Old Man died in 1993, at the ripe old age of 99.

Lithuanian

Immigrants from Lithuania alighted on College Street in two distinct waves, leaving their mark by creating two Lithuanian Catholic churches in the area before they dispersed to other parts of the city, taking their parishes with them. Today vestiges of one survive, while the other has been replaced by new row houses on College.

In the early 1920s, Sunday churchgoers walking home from St. Agnes or St. Francis would have been joined by Catholic Lithuanians who attended the same services. But by the early 1930s, Lithuanian Catholics were walking home in the same neighbourhood from their own Catholic church, St. John the Baptist. The parishioners, determined to create a focus for their community, had been successful in buying a small Presbyterian church on the corner of Dundas and Gore Vale (now home to a Spanish-speaking congregation of the same name) they could call their own. For a few years, clusters would also meet in the evenings, after work and on weekends, after returning from their relatively low-paid jobs in sweatshops, construction or the meat-packing plants. They would gather to complete an important task: creating a church hall by painfully digging out the basement of the church by hand! Seven years later, the job was done and the hall was used for a Lithuanian school that taught children their mother tongue, as well as for parish supper and meetings, choir rehearsals and social gatherings for the youth.

Post-Second World War Toronto saw a fresh influx of Lithuanians – most of whom were professionals and intel-

lectuals fleeing the Soviet occupation of their homeland. Unlike the older Lithuanians, these political refugees were displaced persons who were forced to emigrate and did so by coming to Canada, initially by signing contracts to work in mines, forests, hydro projects and farms. Over 5,000 eventually settled in Toronto among the older arrivals in the areas surrounding the church: Dundas, Dovercourt and Bathurst near College Street.

To accommodate the new arrivals, the original St. John's Church was enlarged significantly, so that its Presbyterian origins were no longer recognizable. In part due to the strained relationship between the two immigrant groups, whose outlook and vision for their communities reflected their distinctive social and educational backgrounds, a second Lithuanian parish was established further west on College Street, near Lansdowne.

Resurrection Parish had an uncertain start, holding its first set of masses in the Parkdale Famous Player Theatre and later the College Cinema. Land was purchased at 1015-1023 College Street, east of Gladstone Avenue, but a separate church building was never erected. Given the lack of funds for both, the new Lithuanian immigrants chose to build a Lithuanian Hall with a "temporary" church on the second floor, which then became permanent. Even when funds were available, Resurrection Church elected to buy adjacent properties and turn them into offices for various Lithuanian organizations such as the Scouts, university students or the Lithuanian Credit Union. Today both parishes have moved

far away from their College Street roots, with nary a sign of the Lithuanian presence visible to the new generation of café and restaurant patrons.

Latvian House

The Masonic Order, a popular and powerful fraternal organization in Canada, originally constructed Freemason's Hall in 1910, as a central meeting place for several Toronto lodges. As its largely Anglo-Saxon members moved away from the College Street area, the building lost its original purpose, eventually becoming Latvian Hall, a cultural home to Toronto's Latvian community, in the mid-'60s. The building then housed a library, a credit union and a fraternity; seniors' programs, as well as evening classes for teenagers in Latvian language and culture, were also offered. Although Toronto has the largest concentration of Latvians in Canada, their presence on College Street has been limited to the activities within Latvian House.

More recently, the presence of Latvians on College has virtually come to an end: the massive white sandstone building on College has been replaced as a centre for the Latvian community by the Latvian Canadian Cultural Centre in the east end. Latvian House is now a rental facility that hosts wedding banquets, music concerts and even Irish ceilidh dances.

Polish

Toronto is the "Polish capital" of Canada, and if one wanders to the west end of the city, around Jane and Bloor, or the Junction, the presence of this immigrant group is very visible. So why would residents of College Street regularly walk past Polish Hall on the south side of College, across from the College/Shaw Library? It is true that Sir Casimir Stanislaus Gzowski, the most famous Polish-Canadian immigrant, once built a magnificent estate just south of College, east of Spadina. But when the estate was sold to the City of Toronto, his widow moved to Rosedale. Indeed, the earliest Polish immigrants in Toronto did live in the Ward, alongside other newcomers. But as newer arrivals from Poland settled in Toronto, they tended to live further west toward the Junction, working in foundries and the meat-packing industry.

The location of the hall on College Street was central to two groups of Polish immigrants: those who gathered around St. Stanislaus' Kostka on Denison Avenue and those who attended the Church of the Nativity of the Blessed Virgin of Czestochowa on Davenport Road. Today there is little to remind us of the Polish presence on College Street; the old Polish Hall is now the popular club Revival and is frequented, as are other restaurants in the area, by a multiplicity of peoples from all over the city.

Ukrainian

The earliest Ukrainian immigrants, referred to as Ruthenians until the 1920s, first settled either in the Ward, on streets such as Terauley (now Bay), Alice (where the Eaton's Centre is today), Elizabeth and Elm, or the Junction area in west Toronto. After the First World War, the community started to move west along Queen Street, but with an axis at Bathurst. This area became the centre of the Ukrainian community in Toronto between 1920 and the 1960s. Streets such as Denison, Augusta, Lippincott and, further west, Palmerston and Euclid were heavily populated by Ukrainians who bought, rented or boarded in these locales. Major organizations and churches also located here.

The majority of Ukrainians are Orthodox by religion, while the minority are Eastern-Rite Catholic. In Toronto, the situation is reversed so that the majority are Ukrainian Catholics, while the minority are Orthodox. While the Catholic churches are located in the Junction, visitors to the College Street area and hospital patients at the Toronto Western Hospital can stop to look at a beautiful building constructed in the Byzantine style on Bathurst, north of Dundas. In 1938, after years of sharing space with other groups, the Ukrainian Orthodox community moved into its own building on Bathurst. The present church was opened in 1948 and was soon elevated to the rank of cathedral. It hosts a variety of activities, including a music school, a choir and a

Photo: Francis Crescia

Joe Pantalone

Few people are more closely associated with the Little Italy community than Joe Pantalone. As the local city councillor for over 25 years, he has become a familiar figure, staying close to the community while bustling around the neighbourhood on his way to countless community meetings and through the office hours he keeps on Saturday mornings at the CHIN building.

Born in Racalmuto, Sicily, Pantalone remembers arriving in Toronto as a 13-year-old and being driven downtown from the airport. Seeing that the verandas of many of the houses had pinnacles on them, like Sicilian mausoleums, he thought he was passing a cemetery.

He soon enlivened things with his trademark energy. Coming to Toronto without being able to speak English was difficult, but two years after arriving he joined the NDP and by his last year of high school he was student council president.

At 19, he was treasurer of the local NDP, and at 22, while completing an Honours BA in Geography at the University of Toronto, he ran for the office of alderman. He lost four elections in a row before finally gaining office in 1980.

With over 25 years in public life, he is one of the longest-serving councillors at City Hall. As the city's Tree Advocate, he has campaigned for a greener and cleaner Toronto and as Deputy Mayor he has represented the city in many fields.

Ukrainian language school. In 2006, St. Volodymyr Ukrainian Orthodox Cathedral, as it is now known, celebrates its 80th anniversary.

Further up on Bathurst, just to the north of King Edward School, is the Ukrainian Full Gospel Church – a humble building with no distinguishing element on its facade. A few years ago, one would have also seen the Ukrainian Labour Temple, which was established in 1921 and moved to its home at 300 Bathurst Street in 1927. Today, its striking red facade signifies its new use, as the Ching Kuo Buddhist Temple, a transformation that reflects the continuous evolution of the neighbourhood as it welcomes and hosts successive waves of immigrant groups who, as a first act of planting roots in

a new land, establish religious and cultural centres to afford themselves solace and support.

On College Street proper, the Ukrainian National Federation Hall, first situated at Shaw and College, moved in 1932 to 297 College, near Spadina. For 50 years, the UNF was a hub of activity: concerts, banquets, Sunday-night dances, fashion shows, conferences and conventions. In the days of Caravan, the city's first multicultural festival, the UNF's Kiev Pavilion was wildly popular and the lines to get in stretched along College. Children could attend Ukrainian primary and secondary school or participate in a dance ensemble, or a drama or soccer club. The hall was home to a variety of veterans, youth's and women's groups, as well as the Ukrainian

Credit Union, which opened its doors in 1944. A library was also started in the 1940s and went on to become one of the largest in Toronto. At its closing ceremony in 2002, memories were shared of the old men smoking and playing cards in the front room and the recess from Ukrainian School, when students could get chips and pop from the concession in the smoking room. Today the building is quiet, having given way to a Zen Buddhist temple.

Hungarian

In the 1930s, College Street was the northern limit of a lively Hungarian presence in Toronto that saw a community consisting of boarding houses, grocery stores, steamship agencies, churches and clubs. One would never know it today, as the area south to Queen, east to McCaul and west to Spadina is now home to a very different ethnic group. Perhaps because of its proximity, the original Toronto Hungarian House, located at 245 College, was purchased in 1942 as a meeting place for the Toronto Independent United Hungarian Society. Following the Second World War and during the 1956 revolution in Hungary, it became a centre for relief programs to assist Hungarian refugees. Hungarian displaced persons who came to Canada after the Second World War were well-educated and many had established careers when they left their homeland. They were politically conscious and placed great emphasis on educating the second generation in their language and heritage through Saturday language schools, for example. But by the late 1960s, it was clear that Toronto Hungarian House did not have enough space to accommodate the needs of the thousands of Hungarian immigrants who had now settled in the city. Accordingly, a larger building, the

Hungarian-Canadian Cultural Centre on St. Clair Avenue West, became the central meeting place and organizational centre for the three waves of Hungarian immigrants to Toronto, leaving only a historic trace of their presence in the College Street neighbourhood.

The transformation of College Street

As those who live around College Street or visit it will attest, this typically Torontonian thoroughfare, which boasts one of the few remaining streetcar lines in the city, is a microcosm of the many essential elements that represent the success of Toronto. From Yonge Street, where the upscale College Park complex has been reinvigorated by the opening of the Carlu, an Art Moderne special-events venue, past the refurbished hospital buildings, and gliding by the open green space of the Ontario Legislature, the 506 streetcar picks up and drops off University of Toronto students on its way toward Spadina Avenue. Easing its way amid the car and bicycle traffic flowing from Kensington Market, it passes one of the oldest churches in Toronto toward Bathurst Street and enters Little Italy, an area given its character by an ethnic group that has now relinquished the territory to others who will make it their own. It meanders along a working-class commercial strip and residential area that is home to immigrants who have recently arrived or who have chosen to stay, and then gradually leaves College Street on its way to the High Park loop.

Now a densely built urban environment, College Street remains a destination for many Torontonians who come to visit for a while – maybe to a hospital, to Queen's Park, for a class at the University of Toronto, to sip a coffee at one of its fashionable cafés or enjoy a meal at one of the many well-known restaurants – and then leave for their homes in different parts of the city and the suburbs. For others, especially the affluent professional and upper middle class, College Street is a point of arrival, one that redefines the area as it mutates from its immigrant, working-class roots. They covet the residential neighbourhoods that stretch north and south of College Street for their close proximity to the downtown theatre and arts districts, commercial and shopping centres, and walking distances to all variety of amenities.

Gentrification has given the streets and laneways a new look that one-time residents would not recognize as the tree-lined streets in which they and their working-class neighbours raised families and crossed language and cultural barriers. Indeed, it may be the case that some of the new arrivals are the sons and daughters, or grandsons or granddaughters, of those early immigrants – Italians, Jews, Poles, Lithuanians, Latvians, Irish, Hungarians or Ukrainians – who left their traces behind on College Street.

So what

Fetish

Legba-Congo
Legba-Petro ‡‡
Egba-Nago ‡‡
On-Croix

Miles: T
Max Ro

All-Blues

Kind of Blue

Max Roach

Roland Jean, painter and designer, sitting in front of his own paintings
on the set of the film *A Love Supreme*. Photo: Rick O'Brien

The Arts on College Street

BEATRIZ HAUSNER

Conceived as a boulevard to give access to the mansions of Toronto's Upper Canadian elite, College Street was laid in the 1870s. Of the cultural life that went on inside those mansions, before their residents moved north to Rosedale, almost nothing is known: their reading habits, the music they played and dances they danced remained confined to those English-style country homes, well removed from the boulevard that provided them with physical access.

The early years of College Street were devoted primarily to building and commerce, with virtually no room left over for artistic development. In this context, one of the principal manifestations of culture would have been street entertainers and buskers. Joe Ferrari, an Italian immigrant organ grinder, began playing around Toronto in 1912. His weekly itinerary would take him into the College neighbourhood, where, with his 700-pound instrument, he played popular tunes like "Oh, By Gee, By Gosh, Oh, By Jingo" for regular customers who would toss coins at him. To the delight of his listeners, Ferrari worked with a monkey, at least until 1932, when the animal was apparently put down by the police for biting a listener.

College Street comes vividly to life in the memories of painter Murray Laufer. Laufer was born at the Grace Hospital on College, where the Centre for Addiction and Mental Health is today, and lived on Beverley just a few doors south of College. A tour with Laufer along College Street, from Yonge to Bathurst, allows for a series of snapshots through the 1930s and '40s.

A child of working-class immigrants, Laufer would not have had access to the Eaton Auditorium and the elegant Round Room restaurant, located on the seventh floor of Eaton's College Street. Described as "an Art Moderne masterpiece," and the heart of Toronto's cultural life for many years, Eaton Auditorium played host to the major performers of the day, including Billie Holiday, Duke Ellington, Frank Sinatra and the National Ballet of Canada. Pianist Glenn Gould was very fond of the auditorium's excellent acoustics and used the hall for several of his recordings.

Across the street from Eaton's on College, Laufer recalls, "were the Ward-Price Galleries, an auction house. Right behind it was Grenville Street, where Fred Varley of the Group of Seven lived." Walking westward, Laufer recalls passing the Conservatory of Music at College and University, and being wrapped in the sounds of piano music and voice pouring out onto the street. Like everyone growing up in the neighbourhood before the 1970s, Laufer was an assiduous patron of Boys and Girls House, located immediately north of the Toronto Public Library's Central branch at College and St. George. "It was a place full of wonders," he recalls. "In the form of stories, certainly, but also illustrations."

During his high school years at Harbord Collegiate, Laufer remembers "hanging out" at Sammy's and going to the movies at the Playhouse Theatre, both on College. But his fondest moments he reserves for Becker's Delicatessen on College, which he visited well into his years at art school with his friends, who agreed with him that it served "the most wonderful pastrami with hot sauce...." He often ate at the Crescent Grill at College and Spadina. "Next to it was the Homestead Restaurant, which was frequented by an older generation of artists, including Jack Nichols, and the comedian Lou Jacobi."

Avrom Isaacs, Canada's pre-eminent art dealer of the 1960s and '70s, lived in the neighbourhood as a boy too. He launched the careers of artists John Meredith, Graham Coughtry, Michael Snow, Greg Curnoe, Mark Prent and Joyce Wieland, to name a few. Isaacs recalls his first meeting with Robert Markle, another artist who defined that remarkable generation: "He made his living painting advertising signs saying things like 'Lettuce 10 cents a bunch' for grocery stores on College Street." Isaacs came to Toronto from Winnipeg in 1941 with his family. In the beginning, his father rented rooms for the family on Palmerston Boulevard, just north of College. There was no kitchen in the house, so the family ate daily at the affordable Roumanian Restaurant at College and Palmerston. The main course may have varied slightly, Isaacs recalls, but there was always "a bottle of spitzwater, a bowl of dill pickles and a loaf of rye bread." Life in the neighbourhood during the war years was drab. For entertainment, Isaacs recalls walking up and down College Street, from Spadina to Clinton, with his brother Nathan. "There were a great number of churches and, to me at least, expensive cars," Isaacs says. Among his friends in the neighbourhood was Shirley Faessler, the author of *Everything in the Window* and *A Basket of Apples and Other Stories*.

Reading room inside the old Toronto Central Reference Library (1920). The building at 214 College now houses the University of Toronto bookstore. Photo: TPL

Healey Willan (1880-1968), one of Canada's greatest composers, was the renowne-d parish organist and choir director of St. Mary Magdalene Church on Manning Avenue north of College. Photo: AO

The Toronto Jewish Folk Choir performing with guest singer Paul Robeson. Photo: AO

The Toronto Jewish Folk Choir (TJFC), Canada's oldest continuing Jewish choral group, used to rehearse at 7 Brunswick Avenue, a couple of doors north of College. Originally the Young Socialist Choir, they were forced to disband at the beginning of the First World War. The new TJFC was founded in 1925 by a group of immigrant factory workers who wanted to preserve and disseminate their culture through song. Its annual concerts began in 1926 and remained a mainstay of the neighbourhood into the 1950s. Small in numbers at first, the TJFC featured mainly Yiddish and Hebrew folk songs and operettas and was made up of ordinary working folk, amateurs with strong roots in the socialist currents that informed so much of Toronto's Jewish community. Through the 1930s and '40s, the TJFC grew in size and stature, even performing at Massey Hall in the 1950s.

No cultural profile of College Street and its environs would be complete without Healey Willan. One of Canada's greatest composers, perhaps best known for his religious music, Willan commanded national and international attention as the parish organist and choir director of the St. Mary Magdalene Church for over 46 years. Willan immigrated to Toronto from England upon receiving a personal invitation from the principal to join the Canadian Conservatory of Music in 1913. He was an organist and choirmaster at several churches, including St. Paul's on Bloor Street, but it was at St. Mary Magdalene that Willan found "a sense of home, absolute completion," both through performance and original composition, and through his direction of the St. Mary Magdalene Singers, the renowned choir he founded in 1939.

Another church that figures prominently in the cultural history of College Street is St. Stephen's-in-the-Fields. From 1860 to the end of the Victorian era, the church was a centre of social life, providing weekly religious services to large congregations. In 1927, the Reverend James Edward Ward pioneered broadcasting religious services on radio out of St. Stephen's. The Way of the Spirit aired across Canada, on CFRB and CBC Radio, and around the world, on shortwave radio. Broadcasts continued until 1958, when Ward died. St. Stephen's is well-known for the plays it produced for its

Lux Burlesque
&
Cup Cake Cassidy

The day Toronto's new Sunday cinema bylaw went into effect was the day the city's Victorian sensibility breathed its last breath. The year was 1961 and theatres could finally open their doors to patrons on the Sabbath, and what patrons got – at the Lux Theatre on College, at least – was scandalous history in the making.

On Sunday, May 28, the Lux opened its doors for the city's first Sunday matinee burlesque show. The historical event was headlined by "Cup Cake" Cassidy, a six-foot-tall brunette from New Jersey. Her opening stage performance, lit by purple spotlight, attracted 200 paying customers. Although the mixed crowd of middle-aged men, couples and a dozen or so single women only filled half the venue, the attendance was still above the average of a Saturday matinée. A third of the curious onlookers would leave before the next bill that day – a Western film feature.

Lux's reveal-all offering wasn't so revealing after all, by today's standards at least. Their burlesque entertainers had to wear concealing opaque cloths over their rear ends and nipples. Even their star, Cup Cake, defended the shows by saying it was just a form of entertainment. "Why, you can see more in some of these foreign movies," she said. "I think Toronto people who haven't anything to do on Sunday, particularly immigrants, should be able to see a burlesque show if they want to."

Sadly, Lux's entrance onto the burlesque scene was matched with a quick exit. It was closed by the end of the next year, reopening later under a different name, and providing less racy fare: Greek tragedies.

LEFT: An advertisement for the Lux in *Tab*, a sex and scandal weekly filled with racy stories.

ABOVE: Cup Cake Cassidy, a popular burlesque star.

RIGHT AND OPPOSITE: The Lux Burlesque. Photos: TA

patrons, mostly religious dramas adapted from Ward's radio services. They featured actors like Dora Mavor Moore, theatre professionals who would go on to establish major Canadian institutions in the performing arts. The church continues its theatre tradition today with the award-winning Theatre Gargantua.

Of the many cinemas that came and went on College Street over the years, the Pylon (606 College) merits particular attention. In 1939, with the Second World War looming large in the lives of College Street residents, Ray Lewis established the Pylon, in the process becoming the first female impresario in Toronto to open a theatre. Lewis borrowed the term "pylon" from the beacon lights used in airports to

guide planes to the runway, hoping filmgoers would see her theatre as the city's guide to entertainment. After the war, the Pylon became the city's premier venue for Italian cinema. When it was threatened with demolition in the 1990s, the local community's outcry managed to save this Art Deco/Art Moderne-style landmark by having the city designate it as a heritage site. Among the local entertainers who used the Pylon to stage their plays was the St. Agnes Roman Catholic Church Theatre Group. Started in the 1950s, this ambitious effort at drama production was driven by the church's priest, who organized members of the Italian immigrant community, amateurs all, to keep their native culture alive in the new homeland.

ABOVE: Architect Rocco Maragna as a boy with his father on College Street.

LEFT: Italian music comes to Toronto. Photos courtesy of CHIN.

OPPOSITE: Johnny Lombardi's concert promotion in action. Photo: TA

College Street around Spadina comes vividly to life in the memories of musician Doug Richardson. Between 1951 and 1958, from his early to late teens, Richardson recalls refining his skills as a musician with nightly playing. The bands he played with would start early, performing at teenage dances. Afterwards, they would continue playing at places like Grossman's Tavern and the Silver Dollar. After those bars closed for the night, he would move on to the many after-hours clubs that flourished on and around College. Richardson recalls that these after-hour clubs were always full, with audiences there for the local bands as well as to hear the constant flow of musicians from Detroit and Buffalo who came to perform in Toronto.

Of the many speakeasies that Richardson remembers, one stands out in particular. "It was located in an alley just west of Spadina, off of College, and was a favourite haunt for out-of-town musicians who went to jam there, after performing in mainstream establishments like the Paramount, or the Victory, on Spadina Avenue." Richardson says that the after-hours clubs would get busted regularly, though the police

Athol Murray, the founder of Notre Dame College, is in the Hockey Hall of Fame for creating the Notre Dame Hounds and sending over 100 former students to the National Hockey League. He grew up at 445 Euclid Avenue.

H.W. Art Gallery at 665 College (1948). Photo: JA

didn't always come out winning, as the neighbourhood was also home to a whole generation of exceptional fighters, like Little Arthur King and Danny Webb. Richardson says the corner of Spadina and College – so busy with prostitutes, buskers, hustlers and nightlife of all kinds – was the first beat to be assigned two policemen in Toronto. "School was the jam sessions in that club," Richardson says. He remembers with fondness the night Illinois Jaquet came to jam and arranged to visit Richardson at his home the next day. "He gave me many useful pointers," Richardson says. He also explains that the reason so many musicians "gravitated to College Street" was because of the all-night restaurants there like Sammy's and the Crescent Grill, "where they could get a good meal after playing."

Strictly enforced segregation in 1930s and '40s Toronto meant that established black musical artists like Duke Ellington and Cab Calloway were shut out of better Toronto hotels when performing in town. Instead, they were known to have stayed in "Spee 'n' Dee" homes, or homes of blacks living in the Spadina and Dundas area, which stretched up to College. Drummer Willie Wright once said his mother kicked him and his younger brother out of their room just so Sammy Davis Jr. could have a place to stay when he performed in Toronto.

Certainly, the depth and vibrancy of black culture in Toronto was in no small part due to the United Negro Improvement Association, at 355 College Street. Established

in 1919, the UNIA held dances and concerts, and it was at one those dances that Richardson met his lifelong friend and collaborator writer Barry Callaghan. The UNIA was well-respected for welcoming local black musicians and their fans, especially during those times when mainstream venues would turn local talent away, for fear they would attract their friends and undo the segregrated environment of the clubs. The Harlem Aces, Toronto's first black band of the swing era, played regularly at the UNIA Hall. A recent jazz combo named themselves Band 355, after the address of the UNIA, because they considered themselves graduates of the iconic association.

It is impossible to think of Little Italy arts and culture without Johnny Lombardi. From an early age, he displayed a passion for the two driving forces behind his great accomplishments: journalism and music. When Lombardi came back from the war, he went into the supermarket business, first opening a store at Dundas and Bellwoods. In the 1950s, Lombardi bought the building at 637 College and set up the supermarket in the first floor. The food business gave Lombardi a view into the changing, increasingly diverse face of Toronto. He recognized the trends and saw in them the potential for cultural expression. The opportunity presented itself when a mainstream radio station approached Lombardi with advertising space. Lombardi suggested, instead, that the station give him one hour per week to broadcast, amid the advertisements,

music and cultural programming in Italian. This was the seed that grew to become CHIN Radio. One hour per week was hardly enough to satisfy the hunger for Italian community programming, so Lombardi began to organize concerts in Toronto for Italian musical artists. Over the years, Lombardi was able to fill Massey Hall, Maple Leaf Gardens and other venues with international stars like Rita Pavone, Beniamino Gigli, Domenico Modugno (who popularized the song "Volare") and Umberto Tozzi, to name but a few.

In 1966, Johnny Lombardi finally obtained the licence to launch a fully multicultural, multilingual radio station. In the beginning, CHIN Radio operated out of the second floor, above the supermarket at 637 College. It was not until

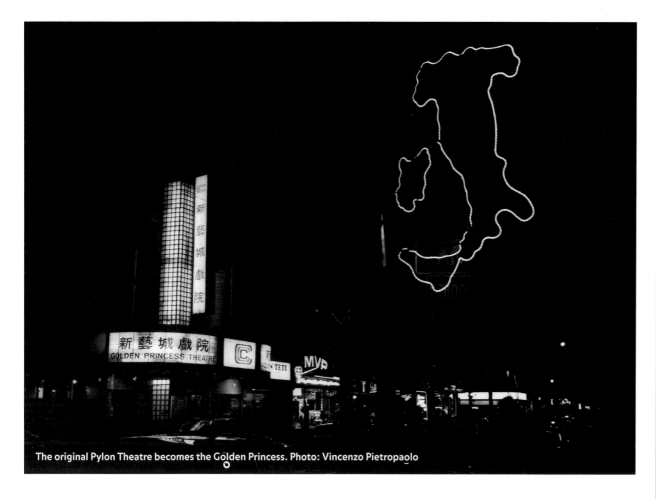

The original Pylon Theatre becomes the Golden Princess. Photo: Vincenzo Pietropaolo

The Pylon Theatre. Photo: Paul French

Ray Lewis

In private, she was Mrs. Joshua Smith, a philanthropist and organizer of charitable efforts and functions for Toronto's high society. In public, she was Ray Lewis, magazine editor, theatre owner, film executive extraordinaire. It was this public persona that brought Lewis her popularity, fame and fortune, in the end.

Née Ray Levinsky, Ray Lewis lived in the middle of the College neighbourhood all her life. As a child, her family lived at 397 Palmerston Avenue, and when she moved out on her own, she lived on Manning Avenue.

Before she became known as the first woman in Toronto to open her own theatre, the Pylon at College and Clinton, Lewis was already in the public eye. She's acknowledged as one of the "pioneer women dramatists" of her era, writing plays at a time when few other women were doing so.

In 1915, a play she wrote and starred in herself (as Ray Levinsky), called *The Other Woman*, ran at Massey Hall and reportedly had a large audience that included many leading arts figures. In the same year, she became the outspoken editor of *Canadian Moving Picture Digest*, and remained at its helm for over 30 years.

Besides writing plays and editing magazines, the prolific Lewis also composed poetry. She sent many of her pieces to the Toronto *Daily Star* throughout the 1920s and '30s.

But of course, her claim to fame rested within the film industry. Besides turning the Pylon into a cinematic mainstay, she even travelled to England in a quest to import British films and actors to Canada in the late 1930s. She successfully brought the famous actress Anna Neagle back to introduce to Canadian audiences for the first time.

Lewis died in July 1954.

1977 that he was able to buy the land across the street, at 622 College, and in 1987 begin construction on the building that houses CHIN today. Lombardi's genius lay in understanding that in order to take culture out of the neighbourhood, one need not leave the neighbourhood, and vice versa. Importantly for College Street, construction of the CHIN building played a key role in the revitalization of the neighbourhood, which had witnessed family businesses along the street closing one after the other, through much of the preceding 15 years.

As a former producer of CHIN's Portuguese programming, Frank Alvarez has contributed greatly to a more open expression of that community's culture. Alvarez sees Lombardi as his role model.

The printed word and its dissemination figure prominently on College Street, from the 1870s to this day. Tradesmen involved in the printing business resided on the street in the 1870s and '80s. Throughout the first quarter of the 20th century, as more and more commercial spaces rose along the street, printing presses and printing shops peppered the street from Spadina to Ossington. A small literary press, Shaw Street Press, was run by writer Cary Fagan and his wife out of their home in the late 1980s. Some addresses, like 357 College Street, appear as fairly permanent venues for printers and publishers. At different points, various outfits could be found here: BH and FM Browns Ltd., College Press, College

OPPOSITE: The Royal Theatre. ABOVE: Cooks at South Side Louie's Photos: Rick O'Brien

LEFT: Cher during the filming of *Moonstruck* at 583 College. Photo courtesy of Teresa and Giuseppe Andaloro

RIGHT: Photos: Rick O'Brien

Street Press, Carroll Galleries, Pond & Stranger Printers, Toronto Typograving Co. Between 1900 and 1915, at the rear of the building was St. Stephen's Church Reading Room. One of the first havens for residents hungry for reading, the Reading Room can be seen, in retrospect, as a kind of public reading space, albeit one that emphasized a specific way of life and set of beliefs.

The first Toronto Public Library branch on College Street opened in June 1900. The building, located at the corner of Brunswick Avenue and College, was leased by the TPL at a cost of $40 per month in the first year. It wasn't until November 1906, however, that the cornerstone for the new central reference library was laid at the northwest corner of College and St. George. Fully owned by the TPL, thanks to a bequest from American steel magnate Andrew Carnegie, the new building became the home of collections and services formerly delivered out of the old Mechanics Institute.

The role TPL has played over time in the cultural development of the neighbourhood cannot be overstated. The building of the College/Shaw branch, for example, signalled an important marker in the life of the neighbourhood. Citizen participation was largely responsible for bringing to the fore the need for a library that could more readily serve the community. Resistance to the initiative from the largely conservative Toronto Public Library Board at the time was finally conquered through political action by local councillor Joe Pantalone who, in the course of a City Hall committee meeting in the winter of 1981-1982, exclaimed: "What, we're good

enough to clean your houses, do your building and repairs.... We should be good enough to have a library too!" As soon as the College and Shaw branch opened for business, it became the 13th-busiest branch in the then 39-branch system.

Bookstores have also dotted College Street over the years. Sid's Magazine Exchange, at 415 College, opened in 1935, at the height of the Depression, and evolved five years later into Sid's Bookstore. Milton Cronenberg, father of film director David Cronenberg, ran a bookshop under his own name at 696 College, in the 1930s and '40s. His niece, the artist Claire Wiseman Wilks, whose family moved into her aunt Esther Cronenberg's house until they bought a place on Montrose, remembers "Uncle Tony's" bookstore well: "He sold magazines, books, including the Blue Detective series." By then, Wiseman Wilks recalls, "the Professor," as Cronenberg was known in the neighbourhood, had started writing articles about stamps for the Toronto *Telegram*. During the three or so years she was a patient at the Western Sanatorium, Milton Cronenberg often came to visit. On one such visit he brought her the gift of a record player, along with jazz records, both of which Cronenberg had purchased next door to his, at Sam Sniderman's music store.

Contemporary bookshops on College include She Said Boom (372 College), Balfour Books (601) and Dragon Lady Comics (609). However, these are rare occurences in a neighbourhood where, strangely, neither printing presses nor bookshops appear to have played a significant role in its literary or artistic history. Here, that role has been largely

Sam Sniderman "The Record Man"

Before he became "Sam the Record Man," Sam Sniderman was just a young man with a vision for the future whose family happened to have a radio store that would become the grounds for his entrepreneurial growth.

In 1929, when Sam was just 10, the Sniderman family opened a store at 714-716 College Street, right below their home, called Sniderman's Radio Sales and Service. When he hit his teenage years, Sam noticed that a "phonograph craze" was growing, so in 1936 he approached his mother, Captain Gert, and older brother, Sid, with an idea about opening a record department in the family store. And soon enough, the store was renamed Sniderman's Music Hall and boasted the slogan "If Sniderman's do not have the record, no other store has." The two brothers built listening booths for customers to sample music in the store; by the 1950s, they boasted 38 of these original booths.

Business was booming, but it wasn't enough for Sam and Sid. The Toronto scene had started moving further downtown, and so went the Snidermans. The family moved their store down to 347 Yonge Street, and Sam the Record Man quickly became the most recognized and most photographed structure in Canada, with its two-storey-high spinning-records sign.

Despite all his success and his awards for his unmatched contribution to Canadian music, Sam the Record Man remains close to his roots – his store's official corporate name is still the original name of his family's first store, Sniderman Radio Sales and Service Ltd.

Sniderman's Music Hall, the beginning of the Sam the Record Man
retail chain at 714 College. Photo courtesy of Sam Sniderman

CHIN radio host Nicola Navarra and comedian Anilo Danese.
Photo courtesy of Joe Pantalone

assumed by public libraries and, significantly, by bars, pool halls, restaurants and, from the 1970s onward, cafés. The biggest players in the literary development of College have always been the street's wide-ranging, affordable and informal eateries, precursors of the sophisticated cafés and restaurants that today anchor it as a fashionable destination.

The trajectory of literary life on College Street coincides almost exactly with the development of CanLit, the community of writers and publishers that saw its rise in the late 1960s and early '70s. Gerry Shikatani figures prominently among the poets who defined that first generation, not only as part of vibrant, often experimental, writer-publisher collectives like House of Anansi Press and Coach House Press, but as a child of the neighbourhood. Shikatani remembers growing up in a rented flat above a store on the east side of Spadina, across the street from the Crest Grill and, later, the El Mocambo. Shikatani recalls the richness of his interaction with the children of Jewish, Italian and Finnish immigrants. He remembers playing ball with his pals, as the adults

watched, sitting on lawn chairs and wooden crates on the Spadina sidewalk, languishing in the summer heat. His most vivid memories, however, are reserved for the Mediterranean and eastern European food he experienced growing up in the neighbourhood. He remembers shopping for it with his parents in Kensington Market and in the Italian grocery stores that began to spring up along College Street.

During the 1970s and early '80s, the stretch of College between Spadina and Major became a magnet for many people in the arts. Modelled after European *cine clubs*, Cinemalumière, at 290 College, was one of the first repertory theatres in Toronto to show international films, old and new. There was an excitement about the movies that showed there, one that was matched with the general feeling of "live and let live" that pervaded the so-called "flower generation." Godard, Buñuel, Fellini, De Sica, certainly, but also rarer films from Brazil, Africa and eastern Europe found their match in an audience open to new images and sounds. A few doors west was Don Quixote – Spanish restaurant on

Universal Negro Improvement Association

If you go on the Kensington Market walking tour, your starting point is 355 College Street. The old three-storey building used to be a clubhouse, you're told, a popular hangout for the black community in the roaring '20s. The UNIA Hall, as it was called, was so much more than that. It was the headquarters of the Toronto chapter of the Universal Negro Improvement Association and African Communities League.

The chapter had started out as the Coloured Literary Association in 1919. Only later did it opt to become a local branch of UNIA, the organization founded by Marcus Garvey in Jamaica in 1914. At a time when incoming black immigrants had nowhere else to go in the city, UNIA became a social, cultural and political meeting point for the community. It was a space that allowed the community to come alive. Pretty much all of the city's early black pioneers and activists either had a hand in organizing UNIA or came to be involved in it all the same.

Besides putting its resources into community self-help and anti-slavery activities, UNIA also held dances and dinners and musical jams when no place else in the city paid heed to its black citizens. At one point, UNIA boasted several hundred active members.

Photo: Laurence Siegel

the first floor, flamenco club on the second. Don Quixote featured some of the best flamenco musicians and dancers in the world, brought from Spain and catering to a burgeoning community of flamenco aficionados, in the early years under the tutelage of Paula Moreno and, later, in the 1980s, under that of Esmeralda Enrique.

Toronto architect Harry Lay remembers that while at Jarvis Collegiate, he and a group of friends were introduced to the flamenco shows by a fellow student, artist Lupe Rodriguez. A native of Andalusia, the very heartland of flamenco, Rodriguez was not only an accomplished dancer, but entirely immersed in the culture in all its expressions. Lay recalls: "We quickly got used to shuttling between the Mars, or the Bagel, to Don Quixote, closing the evening with cheap eats at the local Hungarian restaurant." With time and the gradual replacement of Iberian Spanish speakers with Latin Americans, flamenco receded somewhat, or was combined with a growing interest in Latin dance. El Rancho, at 430 College, was one of the first clubs to offer Latin music and dance. Today, the Latin beat can be enjoyed at Plaza Flamingo, and further west at College and Shaw, at El Convento Rico, a Latin disco known in part for its Friday midnight drag shows.

An important place for literary expression in the early 1980s was the Free Times Café at 320 College, which was established and is still owned and run by Judy Perly. A visual artist with a keen sense for community building, Perly successfully married her management talents to a strong instinct for what attracts people. Because the restaurant is in a kind of geographic no man's land for eateries, Perly has worked hard at attracting business. In the early 1980s, she opened the back room to literary readings and those lucky enough to partake in the experience were able to listen to the cadences of such legends as George Faludy, Robin Skelton and Dorothy Livesay, as well as younger poets like Roo Borson, Paul Dutton and Anne Michaels. Since the 1990s, as literary activity has moved west to venues closer to Clinton Street, Judy Perly has offered her famous Sunday brunches with all manner of traditional Jewish food, served to the evocative Klezmer sounds of bands like Beyond the Pale, Yiddish Swing and the Flying Bulgar Klezmer Band, led by Little Italy resident David Buchbinder. The Free Times Café has become an important destination in Toronto for those seeking a taste of what the neighbourhood was like in the first half of the 20th century.

Of the eateries, bakeries and delis that fed the imagination of artists who lived in the neighbourhood before the 1980s, the Mars (432 College), the Bagel (285), Caffé Diplomatico (594) and the Riviera Bakery (576) remain, continuing to attract the mixed clientele of years past. The latter is the only Italian bakery remaining in Toronto's downtown core. Rocco Reale started as an apprentice baker for the Comisso Brothers' Vesuvio Bakery. With the help of his wife Rosa Carisena's parents, the couple opened for business in December 1974. The bakery still attracts neighbourhood writers and artists with its espresso coffee, Italian baked goods and breads, especially its Zeppole di San Giuseppe (a pastry

CONTINUED PAGE 146

Photograph, Michael Awad. *College Street,* **excerpt from** *The Entire City Project.*

Singer-songwriter and poet
Joseph Maviglia.

Poet Gianna Patriarca.

Inaugural launch of Mansfield Press
at Bar Italia, 2000. Left to right:
Diana Fitzgerald Bryden, Margaret
Christakos, Denis De Klerck, Ann
Shin, Corrado Paina.
Photo: Laurence Acland

served for St. Joseph's feast) and its special Easter bread, which people line up for on the day of the Easter Procession. Celebrities, especially actors who are in town while filming on location, have frequented Riviera, including Marcello Mastroianni and Cher when she was in the neighbourhood with Norman Jewison filming *Moonstruck*.

The Italian Renaissance of College Street can be said have to started with Rocco Mastrangelo's 1968 opening of Bar Diplomatico. First to offer espresso in a café setting, and blessed with one of the best locations in the city at the northeast corner of College and Clinton, Bar Diplomatico became a magnet not just for Italian immigrants nostalgic for the neighbourhood cafés of Italy, but for artists, writers, singers, architects and university students – especially after Mastrangelo and his brother Paul were able to open a sidewalk patio on Clinton Street. The brothers' successful, though protracted, battle with City Hall for a liquor licence that would allow them to serve alcohol outdoors signalled an important shift in Toronto popular culture. As the neighbourhood evolved, so did Bar Diplomatico, becoming *Café Diplomatico*, complete with jukebox in the back.

While Bar Diplomatico helped kick-start the transformation process of College Street, it was through Eugene Barone that Little Italy's Renaissance became a reality. Barone's trajectory weaves itself effortlessly through three decades, beginning at the Bar Diplomatico, where he worked at first. Barone's prescience lay in understanding that Toronto, and with it, College Street, was evolving rapidly and that, with the exodus of the first wave of Italian immigrants to the

northern suburbs and adjacent towns, a new demographic was beginning to move into the neighbourhood. In the 1980s, when the space immediately east of Diplomatico became available, Barone opened a variety store that in a very real way addressed the needs of the new residents: aside from the usual variety-store items, Milk-Nuts & Things sold upscale imported Italian foods, as well as items that appealed to a more hip clientele, like the *New York Times*. "[This] at a time when you couldn't hail a cab down on College Street, because there were none, so quiet was the street in those days," says Barone. Thanks largely to his ability to forecast trends before they really start, Barone created an environment where both the Italian community and the neighbourhood's new resident artists and young professionals felt at ease.

Among the residents who also contributed to this transformation were Italians who left the neighbourhood with their parents, but were moving back now that they were adults. Together with entrepreneurs like Eugene Barone and Giancarlo Carnevale, these "returnees" included artists like Gianna Patriarca and Joseph Maviglia. Born in Italy, Patriarca immigrated to Canada in 1960 when she was 10. Her family settled in a rented flat on Crawford Street. As soon as they could afford to own their own home, however, the Patriarcas moved north, and Gianna's high school years were lived out in the St. Clair and Landsdowne area. Unlike most of her peers, however, Patriarca could not resist the pull of the old neighbourhood and moved back in 1980, this time with her husband, restaurateur Andrew Milne-Allan.

Patriarca is quick to point out that by that juncture, the

neighbourhood had evolved, and the place was, ironically, more fully Italian than when she had inhabited it as a child. "To me, the neighbourhood has the sense of a small village," Patriarca offers. Her own poetry expresses this feeling of rootedness in College Street: "I think I see my father / leaning on the parking meter / passionately arguing / the soccer scores. / How strange this city / sometimes / it seems so much smaller than all those towns / we came from."

Like Patriarca, poet-singer Joseph Maviglia moved to Little Italy in the 1980s. Here he found his muse, as it were, by tapping into the College Street environs' mixture of cultures and the personal histories of its residents. His first poetry collection, *God Hangs Upside Down*, focused on an Italian immigrant working-class family and included a long poem about College Sreet.

Sometime in 1987, Eugene Barone heard that Bar Italia, an old pool hall at 584 College, wanted to sell. The variety store had had its day, and Barone had tried his hand at partnerships with other restaurateurs and was ready for something new. He sold Milk-Nuts & Things and bought Bar Italia with his wife, Nancy. In the beginning, business was slow, especially early in the morning. Barone changed opening hours slightly, removed some of the pool tables and expanded the café toward the back, hiring Andrew Milne-Allan to design Bar Italia's menu. Soon, Bar Italia became fashionable with local artists, writers and filmmakers, who mixed easily with the old-timers who still came for their espresso and to shoot a couple of rounds of pool. In 1992, Barone bought Capriccio at 580A College Street and introduced live jazz to the business – establishing the idea of a dinner club, which

Ron Sexsmith performing at the Orbit Room. Photo: Rick O'Brien

Orbit Room. Photo: Rick O'Brien

other restaurants in the street have adopted with success. In the 1990s, Giancarlo Carnevale's College Street Bar, at 574 College, became a favoured destination for those who like soul music. Across the street, Ted's Collision & Body Repair brought country, garage and rock 'n' roll.

Barone later moved Bar Italia next door to 582 College, hiring Ralph Giannone to design the two-floor space. Once again, Barone's apt reading of the neighbourhood Zeitgeist proved correct: slick and elegant surroundings, when married to a strong but affordable menu of pastas, sandwiches and, importantly, a masterfully designed bar, made for a comfortable mix among local artists, members of the Italian community and, increasingly, upwardly mobile advertising, film, publishing and television professionals. Novelist and columnist Russell Smith, who lived nearby on Euclid Street

at the time, used Bar Italia daily as a place for writing. He would arrive around 11 a.m., set his laptop computer on table 17 and, fortified by Americano coffee, begin to write: "By noon, Bar Italia was busy and the buzz was uniform enough that I could really get going." Smith wrote part of his novel *Noise* and the story collection *Young Men* at Bar Italia. A few years later, he recalls coming in, being told that he had just missed a book club of women reading *Young Men* who'd come to get a feel for the environment of the stories. "Too bad. It could have made for a scene right out of the book they were immersed in," says Smith.

From the beginning, Eugene Barone and Bar Italia manager Denis De Klerck booked bands and DJs for the upstairs bar. They soon turned Bar Italia into a central venue for literary events. It began with the launch of Knopf's "New

Faces of Fiction," the brainchild of publisher Louise Dennys. The event featured first books by Yann Martel, Ann-Marie MacDonald, Dionne Brand and Gail Anderson-Dargatz, all writers who have since achieved international recognition. Book launches, readings, small press events and literary parties continue to this day at Bar Italia. Out of this environment, Denis De Klerck created Mansfield Press (the publisher of the book at hand). Named after the short street that runs between Manning and Grace at the heart of Little Italy, Mansfield Press has published works by several local writers, including Corrado Paina and Kent Nussey. In his novel *A Love Supreme*, Nussey captures the vibrancy of the scene at Bar Italia with exquisite accuracy, immortalizing many of the characters who hung out regularly at the bar through the latter half of the 1990s. Nussey, who spent eight years in

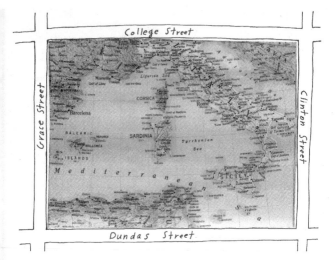

Illustration by Gary Clement (detail) for *Big Deal on College Street* an annual outdoor film festival.

Kingston prior to coming to Toronto, feels that the energy generated by places like Bar Italia and Il Gatto Nero, which he also frequents, is entirely responsible for his having chosen to stay in the city. "It is a real place, a real neighbourhood; it feels like home," he says.

Filmmaker Bruce McDonald, also a resident of the neighbourhood, is currently making a film of *A Love Supreme*, with the help of another well-known Little Italy resident, filmmaker Peter Lynch. Remarking on the circularity of his experience with College Street, Nussey recounts recently bumping into the film crew filming a scene from his book in front of his own house.

People involved in the arts live at ease here, finding stimulation and nurturing among its residents and, importantly, in the establishments they have helped shape and make vibrant. From its early beginnings as a boulevard that gave access to the exclusive mansions of Toronto's elite, through the ebb and flow of immigrants who settled in the neighbourhood and gave shape and renewal to the social and cultural fabric of the street, College has evolved into a veritable cultural hub.

RIGHT: Clinton Street south of College.

OPPOSITE: Bocce players. Photos: Rick O'Brien

Photo Credits

Denis De Klerck and Corrado Paina

A note of thanks

This book was born because of the creativity and passion of many individuals and their enduring love for the "renaissance strip." It would never have seen the light of day without the mentoring and disciplined pragmatism of Joe Pantalone. He was a constant source of insight and ideas, but most of all he introduced us to real places, real stories, real people. We will always be grateful to Joe for being the engine of College Street's renaissance strip, and for having accompanied us as we journeyed through this project.

We would also like to acknowledge the generosity of Barry Fenton, the president of Lanterra Developments, and thank him for his financial help and the many humorous meetings enlivened by his presence and his wit. The Mariano A. Elia Chair has believed in our project since the very beginning and we warmly thank Jana Vizmuller-Zocco for her amazing support and trust.

The project has also had a constant ally in the Gallery of Human Migration led by Rocco Maragna. The Gallery's work in evaluating the impact of the transformational power of migration on Canadian society has been inspiring. Rocco, along with the other members of the fundraising committee (Mayor David Miller, Lenny Lombardi, Barry Fenton, Joe Pantalone, Nick Simone and Peter Aykroyd), has helped us with vision and wisdom.

Mayor David Miller has been a presence throughout the creation of the book, and we will be always grateful for it. This book was definitely begotten by the "year of creativity."

There are also two people who must be recognized because their lives are intertwined with the life and the renaissance of College Street – Little Italy: Lenny Lombardi and Eugene Barone.

We would like to thank all of our sponsors for their financial and in-kind contributions, and in some cases, for their creative input.

Lanterra Developments, Barry Fenton, Lenny Lombardi and CHIN, Little Italy BIA, Manuel DaCosta, Viana Roofing, Grace Meat Market, St. Helen's Meat Packers Ltd., International Brotherhood of Electrical Workers Local 353, Molson Canada, The Centre for Addiction and Mental Health, Tony Natale, Associate broker, Ariston Realty Corp.,

Plazacorp Investments Ltd. Bruno Sinopoli, Mod Club Theatre, Toronto Economic Development Corporation, Alan Vihant, Concord Adex Development Corp., Wittington Properties Ltd., Danny Caranci, Joe Bonavota and Bar Italia, Long & McQuade Musical Instruments, Riviera Bakery, Sicilian Sidewalk Café, Dario Amaral, Eugene & Noelle Barone, George Cominel & Ann Ball, Paul Mitchel & Bonita Brindley, Beate Bowron, David & Shirley Crombie, George Dark, Fiona Chapman & David Pond, Michael de Pencier, Richard Decter, Karen & Stephen Diamond, Theresa & Carmelo Didiano, Robert & Ellen Eisenberg, Tomas Fiore, Roger & Enyd Floyd, Augustino Forgione, Richard Gilbert, Charles Gossage, Joe Centraco & Grace Buttino, Walter & Anne Harhay, Jodel Holdings, Robert & Mary Hunter, Anne Johnston, Michael Kainer, Jassie Khurana, Peter La Farciola, Jill Le Clair, Marcelle & Ralph Lean, Michael & Charlotte Lyons, Michele & Carmela Maccarone, Bruno Marchese, Shinchiro Matsumoto, Judy Matthews, Eduardo & Fatima Meirinhos, Jose & Maria Melo, Michelle Carruthers, Maria Pantalone, Rose Pantalone, Andrew Paton, Richard Peddie, Giuseppe & Francesca Rauti, Marcelina Ponte & Robert Maxwell, Luigi & Gina Santino, Chen Savapak, Mary Sharpe, Chang Shic, Guiseppe Simonetta, M. Sinopoli, Sam Sniderman, Ronald Soskolne, Feodora Steppat, Vince & Raffaela Suppa, Elizabeth Teti, Maureen Whitehead, Neil Wright, Pamela & Edward Youngberg, Minho Roofing Co. Ltd., Il Gatto Nero, CIRC-Radio Inc., Zeidler Partnership/Architects, Trasiti Bar Inc., Café Diplomatico & Restaurant, Bellavista Trattoria & Bar Ltd., Quality Meat Packers, LIUNA Local 183 Training & Rehabilitation Centre – Trust Fund Universal Workers Union Local 183, Toronto Professional Firefighters' Association, DTV Commercial Services Ltd., Bellavista Trattoria & Bar Ltd., Lyric Pond Corporation, Greater Toronto Hotel Association, Malibu Harbourfront Inc., Toronto Construction Association, Landscape Ontario Horticultural Trades Association, P.J. Clephan Ltd., CC Acquisition Corp. Wittington Properties Ltd., Lynda Friendly & Associates Inc., Janet Rosenberg & Associates Landscape Architects Inc., Sam Kotzer Ltd., T/A Samko

Sales, Plaza Corp (Fleet) Holdings Ltd., Viana Roofing & Sheet Metal Ltd., Page & Steele Management Services (1986) Ltd., the Mod Club Theatre, Pasqualino Solo Uomo Ltd., JM Limited Partnership with 1027169 Ontario Limited as General Partner, Ariston Realty Corp., Labourers' International Union of North America Local 506, Hariri Pontarini Architects, Marshall Macklin Monaghan, Joe's Barber Shop, Everlite Luggage Mfg Ltd., Woolfitt's, Mo Dixit & Associates Ltd., Toronto Convention & Visitors Association, Alan Littlewood Architect, Architecture Inc., Key Publishers Company Ltd., Goodman & Carr LLP Barristers and Solicitors; International Brotherhood of Electical Workers L.U. 353, Graziani & Corazza Architects Inc., Sicilian Sidewalk Café Ltd., Regina Pizzeria & Trattoria, Stronco Designs, Stacey Electric Comp.

So many people have contributed to this book with pictures, with writings, with sympathy and kindness, that we run the risk of leaving someone out or identifying them vaguely because we have never known their last names. Our forgetfulness and lack of proper names have only served to remind us of our vivid life here in Little Italy and how easy it is to take it for granted. The following are just a few of the people that have made being here a richer experience.

Manuel and Margherita, Morris Jamal, Steve, Sasha, Oscar and Lucas Donald, Cosimo, Theresa, Alessandra, Gerard and Francesco Mannella, Carlo Basiloni, Vince Bruni, Caroline Christie, David Fraser, Michael Lo Tito, Umberto Manca, Anthony Mancini, Rosario Marchese, Frank Pasqualino, Angela and Pascal Petardi, Roy Pike, Rosa and Rocco Reale, Pierluigi Roi, Donato Santeramo, Lorenzo Vallecchi, Franco Valli, Pina and Filippo Zampino, Humberto Carvalho, the sweet Chinese busker playing in the morning at the northeast corner of College and Grace, Rocco, the Italian homeless guy singing old Italian songs at 5:00 a.m., Judith, Sal at Gatto Nero, Jamie at the Orbit Room, Ali, the eye of CHIN radio, Joe Anile, Martin, Victor, Beth, Davida and Eliot, Steve, Bruno Crescia, Hazel, Steve and Tundra, Erin, Adly Gawad, Mary Pickford, Yvonne, Carolina, Gianna, Andrew and Gia, Emilia, Olivia Chow, Francesco

Galle, Tony, Jenny, Jason and Nathan Barato, the beloved Mario from Porta Aperta (we miss you very much), Grace Bagnato, Father Angelo, Christian Petronio, Albino Silva, Lynn Donoghue (every time we drink espresso, we miss you), Trish Ewanika, Lamberto Tassinari, Giuseppe and Dom Frasca, the Figliano family, Antonia Lanni, Art Eggleton, Father Gregory, Dan Heap, Deborah, Andrea and Luca, Bruno Riga, Tony Ianno, Brothers Bento São José, Nick Mancuso, Fernando Cruz Gomes, Joan Dempsey, Domenico D'Alessandro, Tony Nardi, Alejandro Morales, Sal Manni, Father Melo, Lucio at Gatto Nero, Rick Salutin, Nicholas Campbell, Janet Bellotto, Michael O'Connor, Elizabeth from Salon Teti, Andrew and all of the Pimpinella family from San Francesco Foods, Atom Egoyan, Mario Poretta, Giuseppe Pannozzo, Ted Footman and Dawn, Rocco del Sud, Don McKellar, Shah Alam, Siva, Yoga, Ramesh, Ali and Jahangir, Paul French and Pamela Cuthbert, Michelle, Spencer and Tilda, Carmelo Figliano, Martha Sharpe, Louise Dennys, Richard Gorman, Jeff (he knows), Ian Adams, Tony Swickis, Tony Ambrosi, John Schnier, Robert Fones and Elke Town, Bitondo, Susan Roxborough, John McGrath, Hugh Marsh, Judy Cade, Rocco Galati, Philip Monk, Anne Marie McDonald, Alyssa Palmer, Molly Parker, David Sereda, Peter and Siegrid, Barry Callaghan, Antonio D'Alfonso, Marcello Mastroianni, Shirley MacLaine, John Romano, Andrew of San Francesco, LyricalMyrical publisher Luciano Iacobelli, Valerie Buhajiar, Chantal Aston: the muse of jazz in the roaring years at Capriccio, Joseph Maviglia, Karen Shenfeld, Gaetano Rao, Nuria Enciso, Ollivier Dyens, Domenic, who props up the coffee counter of Bar Italia with Vincenzo, Thomas, Deborah Esch, Carlo, Olindo Romeo Chiocca, Tony Cianciotta, Brian Stillar, Liz Brady, Steven Small, Lisa Klapstock, Paul Mezie, Richárd, Ralph Giannone and Pina Petricone, Pier Giorgio Di Cicco, Zephyr, Clea, and Silas, Margaret Christakos, Peter Boyd, Shah Alam, Angelo Principe, Joe Bonavota, Onofrio, Gabe Caira, Lisa Gabriele, Amy and Johanna McConnell (and Burt!), Zoe, Jerry Berg, Diana Fitzgerald Bryden, Michael Redhill, Noelle Angelina and Luna, Lorraine Segato, Sandra Shamas,

Mashia, Martin Walters, Anna Maria Muccilli, Rob Marra, Steven Surjic, Ann Shin, Fred, Elva, and Emilio Kamiya of El Bodegon for feeding Denis so well for so many years, Maya Dille, Antonio Nicaso, Francesca and Satchel, Roberto Zito, Tony Porretta, David Katulski, Elio Costa, Allan Zweig, Mary, Pat, Tony and nonna, the great people at Balfour Books, Fernando's grocery store, Siderno meat, the Portuguese Taylor, Irpinia Travel, Michael and Carmine and …

We have forgotten many names. We will apologize when we see you on College.

Corrado and Denis

This book is dedicated to Armand, Cecile and Brent De Klerck, and, of course, Spencer.
&
Carlo e Franca Paina, Stefania and Paolo Rampini, Emilia Paina, Deborah, Andrea, Luca, Rita, Plinio, Roy and Dino Verginella and Spencer.

Gallery of Human Migration
Galerie de Migration Humaine

ONTARIO ARTS COUNCIL
CONSEIL DES ARTS DE L'ONTARIO

THE CANADA COUNCIL | LE CONSEIL DES ARTS
FOR THE ARTS | DU CANADA
SINCE 1957 | DEPUIS 1957

MANSFIELD PRESS
A CITY BUILDING BOOK

Writers

Giuliana Colalillo is Professor of Learning Design at Sheridan Institute of Technology and Advanced Learning. Her interest in the history and sociocultural integration of immigrant groups in Toronto , specifically that of the Italian Canadian family, were the focus of both her Masters and Doctoral theses at the University of Toronto. She has written a number of articles on this subject, and most recently contributed a contextual essay on Italians in Toronto for the photography book, Not Paved With Gold (2006).

Denis De Klerck is the publisher of Mansfield Press, which is located on Mansfield Avenue in the heart of Toronto's Little Italy. Mansfield Press publishes poetry and literary fiction, as well as books on community history and urban issues through its imprint City Building Books.

Mark Fram is a determined urbanist: a city-dwelling architectural consultant, urban planner, designer, photographer and essayist. His book Well-Preserved (3rd ed., 2003) is the standard text for historic preservation practice and educational programs in North America. He is a member of the academic communities in the disciplines of both geography and architecture, as both instructor and research scholar, at the University of Toronto. A born-and-bred Torontonian still in his native habitat after travels to faraway places, his preferred mode of transit is walking.

Born in Chile, **Beatriz Hausner** is a poet and author of The Wardrobe Mistress (2003) and translator of some 20 titles of poetry, fiction and children's literature, principally from Spanish into English. Her poetry is rooted in the traditions of Spanish America and international Surrealism. She was President of the Literary Translators' Association of Canada and one of the founders of the Banff International Literary Translation Centre. She works as a public librarian in Toronto.

Domingos Marques was born in Portugal and came to Canada in 1968. After graduating from the University of Toronto, he went on to work as a Vocational Rehabilitation Consultant. He became interested in the history of this ethnic group and co-authored two books: Portuguese Immigrants: 25 Years in Canada (1976) and With Hardened Hands: A Pictorial History of Portuguese Immigration to Canada in the 1950s (1993). As an author and publisher, Domingos also contributed to various publications and published Comunidade, a Portuguese Community newspaper in the 1970s, as well as Silva Magazine in the 1990s.

Manuela Marujo is the Associate Chair for Portuguese at the Department of Spanish and Portuguese of the University of Toronto, from which she holds a PhD in Education. As a resident scholar at the Multicultural History Society of Ontario, Manuela collected oral history and photographs of Portuguese immigrants. In co-authorship with Domingos Marques, she published With Hardened HandsA Pictorial History of Portuguese Immigration to Canada in the 1950s (1993). Manuela has been a community activist in education and a strong advocate for the International Languages Program.

Richard Menkis, a native of Toronto, is an Associate Professor at the University of British Columbia, specializing in modern Jewish history. In 1993, he was the founding editor of the leading journal in the field, Canadian Jewish Studies, and served as editor-in-chief until 2000. He has recently co-edited, with Norman Ravvin, The Canadian Jewish Studies Reader (2004) and is the co-editor, with Harold Troper, of more than 200 entries pertaining to Canada in the forthcoming edition of the Encyclopedia Judaica.

Corrado Paina was born in Milan in 1954 and came to Toronto in 1987. He has published the poetry collections Hoarse Legend and The Dowry of Education with Mansfield Press. In Italy he has published Di Corsa, a collection of short stories, Stolen Time, a collection of poems in collaboration with renowned painter Sandro Martini, and the poetry collection Darsena Inquinata. In early 2006, his novel Tra Rothko e tre finestre was published in Italy, while his latest collection of poetry, The Alphabet of the Traveler, was published in Canada by Mansfield Press. Corrado is the Executive Director of the Italian Chamber of Commerce of Toronto and the editor of the magazine partners.

Gabriele Scardellato was born in San Giuseppe, Treviso, and emigrated to Canada as a child in the mid-'50s. Dr. Scardellato has worked as a director of research resources at the Multicultural History Society of Ontario. He has held the position of Research Fellow in Italian-Canadian Studies for the Mariano A. Elia Chair in Italian Canadian Studies at York University and is currently a contract faculty member of York University. He has published widely both in Canadian ethnic studies as well as in Italian-Canadian immigration history, including Within Our Temple: A History of the Order Sons of Italy of Ontario (1995).

Harold Troper is a professor in the Department of Theory and Policy Studies at the Ontario Institute for Studies in Education at the University of Toronto. He is the author or co-author of many books and articles on the history of Canadian immigration. Among his better known works are Immigrants: A Portrait of the Urban Experience and None Is Too Many: Canada and the Jews of Europe 1933-1945. He has received many honours and awards, including the City of Toronto Book Award and the Sir John A. Macdonald Prize for the best book of Canadian history. He is currently co-Canadian editor for a new edition of the Encyclopedia Judaica and is writing a book about Canadian Jews in the 1960s.

Researchers and Profile writers

Douglas Kwan resides in Toronto, working part-time as a manager of Bar Italia; on other days, he can be found in his studio painting or over-researching an unfinished and/or never to be completed screenplay about disco and baseball.

Emily Saso is managing editor of partners, the Italian Chamber of Commerce of Toronto's official quarterly magazine. She has a masters degree in political science and loves digging through history.

Joyce Thian's contribution to College Street – Little Italy, Toronto's Renaissance Strip included writing many of the profiles scattered throughout the book, photo research and personal interviews. A graduate of Ryerson University's Journalism program, she now combines her lifelong love of writing and teaching by editing educational resources for students and educators aimed at improving literacy.

Featured Photographers

Francis Crescia was born and raised in Little Italy and has grown up in a family that has photography in its blood. Apart from documenting life on the streets of Little Italy, he has worked extensively as a portrait artist, photographing many recognized personalities in entertainment, business, politics and art.

Rick O'Brien is a Toronto-born, Vancouver-raised Newfoundlander. As a photographer, he has been living in and documenting Toronto's Little Italy since 2001. He is currently working as the director of photography for the Bruce McDonald/Peter Lynch film A Love Supreme, which takes place in College Street's Little Italy.

Vincenzo Pietropaolo is a documentary photographer who has been exploring Canada's immigrant subcultures for more than 30 years. His artistry and social commitment have won him widespread recognition and awards. Aside from exhibiting frequently in Canada and abroad, Pietropaolo has published six books of photography, including Canadians at Work and his latest, Not Paved with Gold (2006).

Laurence Siegel has been doing street photography for the past 10 years with particular interest in the personality of neighbourhoods. His work captures the drama of a moment in which people and the space they occupy are connected so that each is expressive. In the past several years, he has displayed his work from the streets around the world at Contact: Toronto Photography Festival. He is a member of Gallery 44 Centre for Contemporary Photography.

Book Design

Bryan Gee is a Toronto designer who lives and works just south of College Street. He has produced award-winning book and editorial design for art galleries, museums and magazines. He was senior designer at Saturday Night Magazine, the Art Gallery of Ontario, and Bruce Mau Design.
His collaboration with Mansfield Press started in 2000 with the design of the first four titles and continues now with the design of this book.

THIS PAGE: Laneways of Little Italy. Photo Rick O'Brien

OVERLEAF: Road collapse on College Street early 1900s Photo: TA